WHEN GOD'S HAND IS ON YOU

Cornelius Lindsey

CONTENTS

INTRODUCTION

I wrote this book for the visionary, the servant, and the lost. My purpose is to share this important and foundational information to help you fulfill the duty you've been assigned. I remember sitting in my room years ago confused and frustrated. I knew God called me for a purpose, but I did not know how to begin. I did not understand it. I sat down with a pastor in his office, and his advice was for me to enroll in a Bible college. I left that meeting more frustrated than I was before. While I understood his answer, I was upset because my desire was not to just know the words of the Author, but to commune with the Author and gain deeper insight than I had before. Could Bible college do that? I would say so. However, that was not my path, and I knew I was destined to take a different one.

I believe God has a journey planned for all of us. He knows exactly what we need and when we need it. He knows where we should go, and He knows how to get us there. The calling He gives us is revealed on the journey He places us. Nothing is wasted along the way. He uses every mess up, setback, and detour to teach us valuable lessons that are needed for our journey. He is with us. No matter if you find yourself hidden in a cave like David, riding in the belly of an ark on flooded waters like Noah, weeping under a juniper tree like Elijah, standing strong like Daniel in the lion's den, or beaten and crucified on a wooden cross like Jesus, you can rest assured that God will not waste any moments of your journey. He will be glorified!

For many years after I began my journey, I felt alone and misunderstood; until I decided to seek for answers. I basically lived in my closet. I sat in there with my Bible and a small lamp. I fasted regularly. During that time, I gave up food and only drank water. I spent many hours in that closet, and my goal was simple—to come face-to-face with God. I wanted Him to encounter me; therefore, I sought Him. I cried out for Him. I asked for Him. I knocked for Him. And He showed up.

I saw many things during that time that would ultimately strengthen my faith. I've endured many tests and trials. I've also encountered demonic forces. These occurrences helped to solidify my faith and trust in God. He never abandoned me through any of them, and I can assure you that He will not abandon you either. I want to share a few of those occurrences and events with you. My hope is that you are encouraged by what you read and comforted in knowing that you are not alone.

During one of my many fasts, I encountered what could have only been a demonic spirit. It was just as real as you reading this book right now. Some would think I was delusional because I had not eaten, but I know what I experienced. My room became so hot that I could see steam rising and I began to sweat profusely. The smell in my room was nothing I had ever smelled before. It was a strong combination of sulfur, trash, the stench of death, and the decay of animals. It was so strong that my nostrils burned each time I inhaled. I tried holding my breath but to no avail. I could not escape it. I stood up on my feet and heard a loud snort as if a raging bull was standing behind me. I could feel it's breath on the back of my neck and saw the silhouette of its image on the wall. I refused to move. I looked straight ahead and pleaded the name of Jesus. I invoked His authority, and everything ceased. A cool breeze entered the room, and the smell was no more. I was shaken from my experience.

I've had many more experiences like that one throughout my life. One time, I hydroplaned off the interstate until a large oak tree stopped my car. It was as if the world stood still as the car flipped and twirled. I saw many of the CDs that had been sitting on my passenger seat flying past my face. My phone was shattered against the passenger side window. I kept my eyes open the entire time. As the car flipped one final time, I grabbed the steering wheel and screamed, "Jesus! Jesus! Jesus! Save me!" I was planted next to a tree within seconds. My door was jammed shut because the impact was on the driver side. I was unable to exit from that side of the car. I had to crawl out the passenger side window to escape. I walked up the hill and turned around to see the damage. As I stood there, a middle-aged bald white man said to me, "Whoever is in that car couldn't have made it!" I turned around, looked at him and said, "I was in that car." As I turned back around to look at the car, he touched me on my shoulder and said, "That means God is not finished with you yet. He has more required of you." I started to weep because I knew it, but I was running from it. I couldn't understand why all of that happened, but I'm glad it did.

The police finally arrived on the scene. Firemen sprayed the car down to prepare it to be taken away by the tow truck. One of the firemen walked over to me and said, "Hey, how did you get out of that car?" I told him I climbed out the window. He said that I was lucky because the car should have blown up. He explained that it was leaking both gas and oil and that the only reason it didn't blow up was because the car shut off. He speculated that it must have shut off the moment I made impact. He was dumbfounded when I told him that the car did not stop. In fact, I turned the car off and shut down the radio. This was significant because he did not believe the car was still running. But I assured him that it was indeed running. My primary piece of evidence was that I turned off the radio. He was dumbfounded, and I knew he did not believe me. He said to the police officer, "You might want to have his head checked. He might have a concussion." Everyone was shocked that I was up and walking without a scratch on my body.

The final shocking aspect of this experience was the man I met when I walked up the hill. The police officer asked me if anyone else experienced the crash. I told him that mine was the only car on the road at that moment, which is very unusual for an Atlanta interstate. I remembered the man I met at the top of the hill and told the officer about him. He told me, "Sir, no one was here when we pulled up. No one saw anyone around you or this area. We were the first to arrive on the scene." I explained to the officer who I saw and provided a description. He was adamant that I needed to go to the hospital, but I knew in that moment that God was calling for me to pay attention.

There may have been many moments in your life where you knew God was getting your attention. He was sharing something with you and opening your eyes to what was to come. I admonish you not to run from it. Realize now that God's hand is on you. He's touched you for His glory.

The purpose of this book is to share some of my journey with you and to share some important insights I have learned along the way. It is my hope that you are encouraged and enlightened by what you read. There are nations awaiting your obedience. Children across the globe are waiting for you to say "yes" to God. The abused and mistreated are waiting for you to leave the familiar and reach out to them. They want and need to hear the Gospel. The lost and blind are waiting for you to fulfill God's destiny for your life right now. It's time. It's time. And I'm excited to be a part of this journey with you. May God bless you and keep you all the days of your life.

-Cornelius

MARKED BY GOD

To know God has called you is to know that He has marked you for His specific purpose. You are set apart from the rest of humanity. No other person in this world has your distinct handprint. You are unique and significant. Luke 12:7 reads that the very hairs on your head are all numbered. They are not counted, which would be remarkable. But, they are numbered! This means God is fully aware which strand of hair is caught in your hairbrush. He knows that hair follicle 1,345,876 will release the hair within it on a predetermined day. He is not surprised by it.

He is aware of who you are and who you are becoming because He created you in His image. He formed and fashioned you in His likeness. No one else in the history of mankind has what you have and can offer what He has put inside of you. If He wanted someone else to do the job or fulfill the task that you have been assigned, then He would have created him or her to do it. But, He chose you!

He knew your insecurities before you thought of them. He knew you in your mother's womb. Before you were a twinkle in your father's eye as he gazed into the eyes of your mother on a cold, rainy night, He already set you apart and aside for His use. Like Jeremiah, He knew and approved of you before He formed you in the womb. Imagine the hands of the Creator of all creation sculpting you in the way He desired—for His purpose. He made no mistakes in how He formed you. He chose you as His instrument and consecrated you for His work. There is no way you could ever fit in with the clubs and cliques that surround you. You are special and holy as He is holy.

You probably have tried to fit into society's mold since your younger years, and have always felt like an outcast. That is because you are an outcast! And there is nothing wrong with being one. There is absolutely nothing wrong with being set apart and different. In fact, I believe that different can be a great thing. You should not desire to be ordinary. There is no life in that. It can be easy to fall into a standard routine that says go to school, get a degree, get a job, get married, have children, and keep working until you are able to retire. But, I believe God has called you for more than that. If we are truly aliens in this world, then we should never get comfortable in the status quo! I have never felt comfortable in it. I have always felt different— like the small dot outside of the main line on a graph. Yes, I was the outlier. For years, I tried to fit into the world's mold, but it would not work! Thankfully, God had His hand on me, and He has His hand on you as well. He will build a wall around you where you do not find any fulfillment in anything but Him. Just like a child would feel without his parents, you will feel out of place and uncomfortable in any place where God is not present. This is because no man has encountered God and lived like he hasn't.

Before moving on with this book, I want to encourage you to put it down for the second and look at your handprint. It's unique and special. No one else in this world has it. God did that. If He would consider that small of a detail, then why would He desire for you to fit in with the world? Make a pledge right now to accept that you are an outcast, and settle in your heart that you are okay with being different.

Even when you feel outnumbered, His presence is enough to make the world's army shiver. Even when you feel alone, one touch from His mighty hand will put you in a state of complete peace. When you are afraid, He is the soft voice that whispers in your ear to calm your nerves. When agitated, He is the soft, cool breeze that brushes across your neck as a reminder that He has not abandoned you.

Understand who you are and who has marked you! You have not just been touched by some mere man. His one touch will outdo a million hands of men. You could lay flat at the altar as one thousand priests pour oil all over your body, but it means nothing if the God who created all things does not touch your heart and compel it to do as He directs.

The greatest achievement for mankind doubles as a great mystery for many. It isn't the moment man set foot on the moon or the moment black gold was pillaged from the earth. It wasn't the moment Noah floated with his family in the safety of the ark or the day David was crowned king. The greatest moment in our world's history is the day Jesus Christ paid the price for our sins. It was on that day that cold, callous, and spiritually dead men were given the opportunity to live. For each of us, the greatest day of our young lives was the day our eyes were opened to the truth, and we passed from death to life. It was when our old nature was put to rest, and our new nature emerged with life eternal.

It's commonly said that the two most important days of a man's life are the day he was born and the day he realizes why. Well, I add to that statement that the greatest day of a man's life is the day he's born again— fully passing from death to life—and the second day is the moment he realizes that he's living in a graveyard of potential. The moment you realize that you've been reborn with life to give life to everything and everyone that's dead around you, in that moment your entire life will change because your eyes will be open to an undeniable reality.

You were born to impact this generation at this time for His glory. He created and placed you in a valley of very dry bones. He has called you to prophesy to those bones so they might live. He's purposed you to uplift and change a dying city, revitalize a failing community, edify a broken people, and preach life to dead beings. He called you to ministry with His qualifications. This is because no earthly merits could qualify you for what you are called to do. Only God can touch and equip you for His work. Therefore, you cannot do what others do. He set your journey straight. Only you could walk the path He designed. The shoes He has equipped for you are designed to fit only your feet. He enlisted you; therefore, only He can train you as He desires.

The apostle Paul makes a striking claim. He makes it clear to the Church in Galatia that he has been crucified with Christ and bears in his body the wounds of the Lord. He is not referring to a tattoo on his body, but a brand stamped onto his heart. It wasn't an outward crucifixion, but an inward one. He was devoted to the task of establishing churches and spreading the Gospel amongst the Gentiles. No other task burdened his heart more than that. You can learn a lot from Paul's devotion. It is for sure that he out-prayed and out-passioned the others. "One thing I do," he said. Those are words of focus and precision. He makes it clear that he is marked inwardly with a task that cannot be denied. It is the reason he breathes, and his desire is to fulfill his assignment before going to his grave. He accepted his calling inwardly and answered with confidence outwardly! His devotion was so strong that no physical, social, or personal attack could dissuade him from accomplishing his purpose. He was committed! We can learn from that example.

He was separated to spirituality and strict devotion to Christ. His faith was sure, and his discipline was paramount. It didn't matter if he was unwelcomed by the people, unloved by his enemies, unsponsored by the chief priests, or unmatched by the other apostles. That made little difference to him. He did not seek honor for his deeds or accolades for his accomplishments. In fact, the fulfillment of his duty was enough.

Read carefully the words from 2 Corinthians 11:16-33.

> *Again I say, don't think that I am a fool to talk like this. But even if you do, listen to me, as you would to a foolish person, while I also boast a little. Such boasting is not from the Lord, but I am acting like a fool. After all, you think you are so wise, but you enjoy putting up with fools! You put up with it when someone enslaves you, takes everything you have, takes advantage of you, tasks control of everything, and slaps you in the face. I'm ashamed to say that we've been too "weak" to do that! But whatever they dare to boast about—I'm talking*

like a fool again—I dare to boast about it, too. Are they Hebrews? So am I. Are they Israelites? So am I. Are they descendants of Abraham? So am I. Are they servants of Christ? I know I sound like a madman, but I have served him far more! I have worked harder, and faced death again and again. Five different times the Jewish leaders gave me thirty-nine lashes. Three times I was beaten with rods. Once I was stoned. Three times I was shipwrecked. Once I spent a whole night and day adrift at sea. I have traveled on many long journeys. I have faced danger from rivers and from robbers. I have faced danger from my own people, the Jews, as well as from the Gentiles. I have faced danger from men who claim to be believers but are not. I have worked hard and long, enduring many sleepless nights. I have been hungry and thirsty and have often gone without food. I have shivered in the cold, without enough clothing to keep me warm. Then, besides all this, I have the daily burden of my concern for all the churches. Who is weak without my feeling that weakness? Who is led astray, and I do not burn with anger? If I must boast, I would rather boast about the things that show how weak I am. God, the Father of our Lord Jesus, who is worthy of eternal praise, knows I am not lying. When I was in Damascus, the governor under King Aretas kept guards at the city gates to catch me. I had to be lowered in a basket through a window in the city wall to escape from him.

Paul was branded; therefore, he was willing to endure all for the cause of Christ. Can you say that? Are you willing to go hungry, endure sleepless nights, be burdened for the church, be persecuted, abandoned, whipped, bitten, cursed, and left for dead? Are you willing to walk away from the many worldly opportunities presented to you and every jewel of earthly honor for the cause of Christ? Are you willing to reject the lure of worldly success and applause? Are you willing to be blind to the ease of comfort? Are you willing to be deaf to the siren-like voice that screams for you to run back to the sin you once loved and abandon the call? If you're not ready for this, then this may very well be where your journey ends! However, if you are ready, then prepare for a journey of epic proportions!

Paul was clearly identified by his humility, suffering, service, and passion. He was only focused on walking in the center of God's will, and he refused to step outside of it to the point of death. He walked a tightrope of obedience to finish the call he was given. Christ ignited a flame in his heart, and he kept it burning until he entered the grave. Jesus made a home in his heart, as He does with you. Paul endured famine, peril, the sword, nakedness, ridicule, persecution, distress, and tribulation. Still, he said he was the least of the apostles. What a man! He was marked! And you must be marked by God in order to fulfill your assignment.

The very fact that you are reading this book should tell you that you are marked. I believe God is pricking your heart at this very moment. He is prompting you to make some decisions right now about your life. There are some things you need to let go and some relationships you need to release. The best way, I believe, to know what to let go of and what to release is through confirmation from the Holy Spirit. Some things are apparent. Either those around you are compelling you to do ungodly things, or there is little to no edification. Also, there are some things that seem to be prosperous or beneficial. They look like doors that we should walk through. They even look like answered prayer but do not get too comfortable because God could require you to release it. I'm compelled in this very moment to persuade you to let go of whatever it is He is prompting you to remove right now. It must happen. You're branded, and God is compelling you to do it because it is what He expects of you. I see more Christians sporting their tattoos, fraternal organizations, and clothing brands more than the brand of Christ. And you sport His brand by the way you live your life. Please don't misunderstand me. Although I am not a fan of tattoos, I do not condemn anyone who has one. In fact, I don't have a heaven or a hell to sentence anyone to. You can wear whatever clothes you want. Just don't allow them to outshine the mark of Christ on your heart. If the brands you wear are more valuable than the life you live, then the brands are your god. They must be removed! Remember who you are and why you have been called!

Before going to the next chapter, remove what needs to be moved. It's time to clean house in preparation for a journey of epic proportions.

BEING CALLED

Ministry is not a performance. It is not a social media spectacle designed to bring you glory. It is a noble calling. One that God does not take lightly. We are supplied with an eternal message of hope and redemption and tasked to take it to every corner of the world. We are given the responsibility of edifying our brothers and sisters, so they are strong enough to fight the good fight of faith and endure their journey until the end. Ministry is not about filling up conference rooms or stadiums. It is not about amassing a large social media following. It is more than a 45-minute, well-organized sermon on a Sunday morning. It is a life of service dedicated to an eternal cause that is much bigger than you.

By the grace of God, I will answer three questions in this chapter: What is ministry? How do I know I am called? And, how do I begin? I began my search for the answers to these three questions back in 2007 when the burden of ministry was implanted in my heart. Many years later, I am able to answer these questions with confidence. And, it is my prayer that you will find what you need from what you are about to read concerning ministry.

WHAT IS MINISTRY?

Many manage to complicate the simplicity of what ministry is. Oftentimes, we hear what it is not. That ministry is not just great charisma to preach a sermon in front of a large crowd or traveling to a foreign country to take pictures with the poor and needy. Let me put it simply. Ministry is servanthood.

The word "ministry" is derived from the Greek word *diakoneo*, which means to serve. It involves our service to God and others, and all service requires sacrifice. An effective servant is selfless so he can focus on assisting others. If he is full of himself, he will be ineffective in serving those under his care. Jesus provides the best demonstration and example of service we should follow. In Matthew 20:28 we read these words: "For even the Son of Man came not to be served but to serve others and to give his life as a ransom for many." There are two main themes in this verse—service, and sacrifice. Ministry involves the willingness to serve God and others out of love. It also means sacrifice, which is the surrendering of self as an offering to God. We minister to God and others through the preaching of the Word of God, by meeting people's needs, evangelizing the lost, and serving one another. Some would consider these actions as 'going into ministry.'

This is the concept that is often spoken about in religious circles. They assume their actions alone will define and validate their call of ministry. This is dangerous because someone could think that doing things 'for' God means that he is being effective. That is not true. Consider Luke 18:11-12. Jesus is confronted by some self-important people, and he tells the parable of an arrogant Pharisee. Jesus describes the attitude of the man like this, "The Pharisee stood by himself and prayed this prayer: 'I thank you, God, that I am not a sinner like everyone else. For I don't cheat, I don't sin, and I don't commit adultery. I am certainly not like that tax collector! I fast twice a week, and I give you a tenth of my income.'" Jesus finishes his lesson and responds to his hearers in verse 14 saying, "I tell you, this sinner, not the Pharisee, returned home justified before God. For those who exalt themselves will be humbled, and those who humble themselves will be exalted."

The Pharisee mentions things he has done for God, but it is evident that he has really done these things for himself. While he thinks he will be rewarded for it, he will not. He has already received his reward, and it is earthly and fleeting. In relation to ministry, trying to do things for God will never replace who you are in Him. For this reason, I shy away from the phrase 'going into ministry.'

I do not prefer the phrase because it suggests that ministry is a destination, vehicle, or a list of good deeds or tasks to accomplish. Instead of telling people that I am going into ministry, I like to say that ministry is growing within me. There is a big difference between the two. Going into ministry suggests that I need to do something. Ministry growing within me suggests that I am developing as an individual and being prepared for service. We must never forget that we are human beings, not human doings. What we do is an expression of who we are within. So, if we desire to change our actions, we must first renew our mind. Salvation is an inside job that flows outwardly. Therefore, who I am will control what I do.

This is precisely why God focuses on the heart (1 Samuel 16:7). It is truly the focal point of God's work of transformation. The most important question to ask is, "what is growing within me? "I believe that question is most clearly answered in Galatians 5:22-23, which reads, "But the Holy Spirit produces this kind of fruit in our lives: love, joy, peace, patience, kindness, goodness, faithfulness, gentleness, and self-control. There is no law against these things!" If ministry is defined as service, then we must make sure the attitude and heart behind what we do are in right alignment. If we are not loving, patient, kind, good, faithful, gentle, and disciplined, our 'ministry' can be tainted and ineffective. As the Holy Spirit matures His fruit within us, we become ripe and ready to serve others.

Effective ministers are Spirit-filled ministers manifesting the fruit of the Spirit. They are effective because their fruit, which is produced by the Holy Spirit, is more valuable to them than their gifts. They understand that great gifts mean little to nothing coming from a vessel of bad fruit and terrible character.

HOW DO I KNOW I AM CALLED?

Your calling to serve began after you were born again. It is the moment after you came to the knowledge of truth, which is knowing and confessing Jesus as Lord and Savior. The seed was planted at that moment of realization. The Holy Spirit planted and began to grow His fruit within you. You began to grow in love, patience, joy, peace, kindness, goodness, faithfulness, gentleness, and discipline.

He also implanted His gifts within you. These gifts are listed in 1 Corinthians 12:8-10. They include wisdom, knowledge of faith, healing, miracles, prophecy, discerning of spirits, speaking in tongues, and interpreting tongues. These gifts are given for the building up of the body of Christ. They are everything you need to be effective in ministry. Each gift is significant and important. Let's look at these gifts briefly.

The gift of prophecy is being able to proclaim a message from God. The gift of tongues is the ability to speak in a foreign language that you do not have previous knowledge of, which allows you to communicate to others who speak that language. The gift of interpreting tongues is the ability to translate the tongues that are spoken and communicate it back to others in your language. The gift of knowledge is the ability to have an in-depth understanding of an issue or situation. The gift of wisdom is the ability to make decisions and provide direction that is in accordance with God's will. The gift of faith is the ability to trust God and encourage others to trust in situations that some would doubt. The gift of healing is the miraculous ability of restoration to a person who is injured, sick, or even deceased. The gift of miracles is the supernatural ability to perform signs and wonders that direct others to God. The gift of administration is the capacity to organize and lead in His church. The gift of helps is the capability and desire to help others by doing whatever is needed to get the job done. These gifts are given by God to be used for His glory in our service to others. These gifts mix with His fruit to create effective ministers.

As these gifts and His fruit develop within you, God allows you to see others as He sees them. You will begin to understand the needs of the people and know how you should respond to them by the leading of the Holy Spirit. For example, God may develop a desire within you to minister to orphans. You will become overwhelmed with the desire to assist those who have been abandoned by their parents or no longer have parents to care for them. It will become such a burden that it becomes the only thing that can fulfill you. The Holy Spirit could give you a gift of helps and faith, which makes it possible for you to do whatever it takes to help the orphans and encourage them to trust in God, no matter their circumstances.

You will not be able to deny the burden God places on your heart for service. And that burden to serve and utilize your gifts in service to others is a clear indication that you have truly been called! You will see people the way He sees them—as those in need of assistance. Where you once saw gaps, God will endow you with the ability to build a bridge so others can walk over the ditch that once separated them from God's purpose for their lives.

I know the burden of being called. For many years, I wrestled with the idea of being called, but I knew I was called to serve as a pastor from an early age. It is as if God whispered it in my ear while I was in my mother's womb. Those words were seared on my heart. I would try to deny it, but I could not. I spent years telling people that I would never pastor a church. I had zero desire to do it. I was pleased with serving as an evangelist, which is a traveling minister. I did not want the responsibility and accountability of pastoring a congregation of people, but God had other plans. God burdened my heart with the desire to see people made whole and grow in the knowledge of the truth. While I felt good traveling the world and preaching the Gospel, it was not fulfilling. I knew God was steering me in another direction and appointing me to a new office—one of pastoral leadership. He gave me visions while I slept, compelled me to start Bible studies, and gave me a passion for looking after His people. I could not deny it. You will not be able to deny it either. When God burdens you with it, you won't be able to deny it. That is confirmation that you have been called to serve. Stop fighting it.

HOW DO I BEGIN?

I believe in allowing things to grow organically. This means your calling is not inflated by unnecessary artificial fillers. What this means is you do not have to do or say things that are outside of the scope of what God is instructing you to do. For example, an apple that is organic begins as a seed in the ground that is watered and allowed to develop naturally. Anything that is not organic is modified in some way. Our fruits and meats are much larger nowadays because they are genetically engineered. They are cheaply produced, which can cause greater risks later on. An organic calling is not forced on you by others. A 'forced calling,' on the other hand is a profession, not necessarily ministry.

A profession usually requires you to get specialized training and teaching so you can perform your job responsibilities for compensation. Professions do not require passion. I believe that ministry is not a profession, but a passion. Professions require the intellect to perform a job well, but a calling of ministry is about passion. The difference is that a profession can be your job to make money, but ministry is the passion you perform for fulfillment. And it is possible to have a profession and also be a minister. Jesus was a carpenter, but His passion was doing the Father's business. His profession was sculpting wood, but His passion was sculpting hearts. The passion is born organically at the time of salvation, and that organic start is the beginning of the call of ministry.

As the pastor of a vibrant church, I do everything I can to produce organic growth. I will not establish a ministry at the church unless God burdens someone's heart with the desire for it. Our church ministries—marriage, children, singles, outreach, and so on—started because God placed the need on someone's heart. He or she approaches me with the vision, and the ministry is born.

How do we know the ministry will be effective? That is a great question. I believe the fruit will prove its effectiveness. Like seeds planted in a fertile garden, you can expect the plant to grow as it should. And, you can expect it to produce more seeds, which ultimately produces more plants that produce more fruit.

You can have other organic associations. I enjoy organic friendships—relationships that grow through mutual respect, encouragement, and a healthy flow of conversation. If it isn't organic, then it feels forced. I like organic conversation, which is an opportunity for two or more people to converse about things that matter to them without any feelings of intimidation or frustration. You can have an organic marriage, organic friendships, organic conversations, and an organic ministry. Allow the Holy Spirit to lead you along the way.

Whatever He creates and guides is organic. He enriches you with His word and guides you with His steady hand. We know from John 15 that He is the Gardener; therefore, you can trust that He has established you and will allow all the works of your hands to develop organically. He does not add anything synthetic to what His hand touches. He does not have to recreate a natural product because everything He creates and guides is natural. He is the prototype. Since your calling comes from Him, it is natural. Since you come from Him, you are natural. You do not have to add anything to make it feel more real or more important.

There are some practical things to consider concerning how you begin in ministry. You can identify the core values of your ministry. Assess your needs and wants. What will the budgetary needs be for the year? I would suggest sitting down with established ministers to discuss what they have done so you can learn how to forecast properly. Establish the vision—where the ministry is headed—and the mission, which is how you will get there. Make sure your needs and the vision are properly aligned so that you can remain focused on fulfilling what God has called you to do.

You can also set short and long-term goals. Determine how many volunteers you need and how you plan to recruit them. Think about your leadership team. How will you establish it? These practical things can help you build upon a solid foundation. Always remember that the foundation is not what you do, but who you are. And who you are is a total of the fruit that identifies you.

Ministry is a lifelong journey. Enjoy it. Allow the fruit the Holy Spirit to grow within you and the gifts He lends to you to affirm your calling.

THE ASPIRATION OF MINISTRY

Going into ministry seems to be one of the common trends in our day. So many young adults spend their waking hours talking about how God is calling them into ministry. I know what those conversations are like because I had many of them. I, like many people today, thought going into ministry was more of a place and a title. I assumed it meant I had to either have a congregation or be a missionary in a foreign land. I assumed it meant I needed to have men lay their hands on my head and anoint me with oil. My biggest mistake was thinking that ministry is something you go into instead of ministry being that which grows within you! In order for us to fully grasp the heaviness and reality of Christian ministry, we must understand what it is and what it isn't, who we are called to serve, why we are called to serve, and how we are called to serve as ministers of the truth.

Ministry is from the Greek word *diakoneo*, which means "to serve." It's also translated from the Greek word *douleuo*, which means "to serve as a slave." Both of those definitions are important for us to understand and know. We are called into ministry, which means we are called into service to our Lord for the benefit of His people and to edify His Body. We do all of this in His power, strength, and ability. Notice in Matthew 20:28 and

John 13:1-17 that Jesus is the standard-bearer for pure ministry. He didn't come to be served, but to serve. This is our example for ministry and one that we must consistently follow.

As ministers, we seek to serve and meet the needs of other people. In doing so, we fulfill the commandments, which are to love the Lord our God will all our heart and to love our neighbor as we love ourselves. Our love is shown in our ministry. It is shown in our graceful actions and bountiful giving. We show that our ministry is truly pure when it is impartial, unconditional, graceful, and merciful. Like Jesus, we seek to serve and help others instead of being served by others.

This concept of ministry can be very difficult for modern-day believers to understand. This is because much of our society today relies on service to self. It focuses on the importance of what it means for self to be served and appreciated. We've coined phrases like self-love and self-esteem that places emphasis on the person instead of looking at how we—even in our brokenness—could serve others.

We've also taken ministry to be more of a profession rather than a way of life. Many assume that ministry is more about what can be done for self rather than what can be done for others. Many also assume that ministry is about the profession or position of the person, such as being a pastor or evangelist, instead of the actual lifestyle of the believer. Because of this seriously warped view of ministry, it has become more of a destination and occupation rather than a sense of revelation of living a life of heartfelt service and dedication to the Lord. Pastors and evangelists are not the only ones who are involved in ministry. In fact, it would be an incomplete view of the word to believe that ministry is just something you do, instead of who you are. Ministry grows within you before you ever step into a specific context to live out who you are in Christ.

Romans 12:3-8 is a great place to look to better understand our Christian service. It's about our dedication to edifying the Body of Christ. We use our gifts, which are bestowed unto us through and by the Holy Spirit, to serve others. We do these things to benefit the greater Body and serve a cause, which is bigger than us. Consider the calling we've received from the Lord. We serve as ministers to fulfill His Great Commission. Jesus spoke these words in Matthew 28:16-20;

> But the eleven disciples proceeded to Galilee, to the mountain which Jesus had designated. When they saw Him, they worshipped Him; but some were doubtful. And Jesus came up and spoke to them, saying, "All authority has been given to Me in heaven and on earth. Go therefore and make disciples of all the nations, baptizing them in the name of the Father and the Son and the Holy Spirit, teaching them to observe all that I commanded you; and lo, I am with you always, even to the end of the age.

What a Commission we've been called to as active and faithful ministers. We live for a greater purpose, which is to snatch lifeless men from an inheritance of hell. We preach life through Christ so those who are dead in sin might live through Christ Jesus. We preach hope to the hopeless and provide help for the helpless. We teach holiness in such a way that immoral men might rise to a higher standard of living and sanctify their polluted hearts. Our call of ministry is eternal, as is the Lord who has called us to serve.

Ministry is not about stages and microphones. It is not about traveling to and from different conferences and events to stand before men and women. It isn't about having a modern logo and fancy website. It's more than that. Because many believe ministry is about public performance, it's become competitive. Once ministry becomes competitive, it ceases to be ministry. It's a travesty to see what ministry has become in our day. Many fight for positions and awards. We've made ministry out to be about earthly appreciation and worldly gain. The number of people in a congregation is used to validate a preacher's calling and serves to inflate his ego. Nowadays, the larger the crowd, the more influential the preacher. Listen to me carefully! That is not how it should be.

The apostle Paul warned Timothy of this very thing in 2 Timothy 4:3. He wrote to him *"For the time will come when they will not endure sound doctrine; but wanting to have their ears tickled, they will accumulate for themselves teachers in accordance to their own desires."* That has happened in our day. You can rest assured that true preaching against sin and calls for repentance will not be met with as much enthusiasm as sermons about earthly prosperity and happiness. The hard-hearted and perverse find comfort in unhealthy doctrine. They will take these words and eat them just like the majority of men and women love to eat unhealthy food. You won't find many people who'd prefer a plate of raw vegetables over a cake that's packed with sugar. The cake tastes great for the time, but its harmful consequences lie in the distance. You may not see the detrimental effects right away, but rest assured that you will see them.

Consider this; sugary sermons give you a sweet tooth for sin. It will have you running towards that which God hates, and in the process, you will be trying to validate your perverse living. The teachers of unhealthy doctrine will convince you that the life of sin you're living is okay and that God is somehow pleased with it. It's a lie from the pit of hell. As ministers, we are called to preach the truth without compromise. Even so, we are called to live out the truth we're called to preach. Our life should exemplify our words. People should see how we live and be encouraged before they hear our words.

The personal life of the minister is just as important as the actions of the minister. Unfortunately, many believe their public actions precede their private worship, but they are mistaken. The private life of the minister is important. We must be qualified to serve. Have you first received a divine calling? Have you truly been called by God and commissioned for His purpose? You can either be called by God or called by man, but there's a big difference. I know ministers whose qualifications include a degree from a prominent university in theological studies and the laying on of hands. Both of these elements can be a part of your journey but consider the weightier matters. Has God laid His hands on you? Has He burdened your heart with passion for a broken generation? I'm not talking about you feeling sorry for a certain situation. I'm referring to God placing such a stamp of burden on your heart that it keeps you up at night. It's one that won't allow you to go to sleep at night. You can't help but weep daily because of the lives you've been called to serve.

There was a sweet, older woman who came to my church. After I had finished preaching, she came to the altar. I stepped down to converse with her. She looked like she had been crying. Her hair was disheveled, and she seemed to be out of it. I inquired what was wrong, and she said she had been up all night crying out to the Lord. She wasn't sure what was happening to her. All she knew is that she had a strong pull on her heart to help women who are considering aborting their babies. She was having dreams about babies and rescuing the young. She felt very strongly about it. She couldn't deny what she was feeling, but she couldn't understand it. I looked her in the eyes and said that God was burdening her heart with a cause that's bigger than her. She couldn't pray that feeling away. It was strong within her. Her calling didn't come inside a classroom. It came through divine intervention. God, Himself, intervened from the heavens and touched her heart. This is what it means to have a divine calling. It's more than a strong desire to help. It's a brokenness, an empathetic pull to deny self and commit your life completely and totally for service unto the Lord. This is why I know I was called to pastoral ministry. I know it's not of myself because I promised myself that I would never be a pastor. I was adamantly against doing it, but God burdened my heart for His people. He put a burden in my heart for my city. It was so intense that I couldn't ignore it.

Those who answer the call of ministry should be spiritually mature. They should be Spirit-filled Christians with a love and passion for serving the broken. I've spoken with men who believe they've been called to a certain aspect of ministry. For them, it was pastoral ministry. They'd tell me how they believed they heard the call from God. Well, I'd look them square in the eyes and say, "Before answering the call, make sure you've counted the cost! This is no light thing. Don't answer the call unless you're left with no other choice but to answer it. If you're not at that point of desperation where all you desire is to please God by answering His call, then walk away from the phone!" Some would assume that my words to those men were disheartening. That was not my objective. I was trying to get them to see, as best as I could, the cost of God's calling. The purpose of my words was to get to the heart of the matter. I wanted those men to know exactly what they were getting themselves into.

I believe that's what is wrong with many of the ministry leaders we have in our day. Many of them assumed themselves into a position without first considering the cost. They didn't consider that the call requires every single bit of them. It doesn't accept half-hearted effort. They can't be lukewarm or lazy. It requires mental and emotional toughness. You must have very thick skin to endure the insults that will be thrown at you as you try and serve. Many don't last because they didn't count the cost. They stepped out of the boat onto the water, noticed the oncoming storm, and sank. They heard the word from God but ran in a different direction when their assignment was too much for them to bear. Some answered the call, but were too enchanted and enticed with the luxuries and comforts of the world. Others were choked by the cares of the world. They started, but they didn't finish. This happens far too often in our world today. I've seen too many churches shut their doors because the pastor is tired or wants to give himself to some other earthly achievement. What stops any minister from quitting ministry can be distilled down into two components: (1) actually being called and (2) spiritual maturity.

The minister is to be spiritually mature. There's no other way around it. He cannot be a new believer because if he is, then he's not spiritually mature! This would also be a direct violation of the qualifications that Paul gave for those who would be ministers in the church (1 Timothy 3:6). He or she should have a sound mind and have the ability to receive wisdom from God. He should be able to communicate effectively in a way that deals with all people, not just those who are easy to deal with. He should be a hard worker and a good steward of his time. He should be impartial in his dealings with God's people so that he is able to care for the entire flock equitably. He is compassionate and displays the works of the Holy Spirit. He cannot be puffed up with pride or arrogance. He invests daily in his spiritual growth and development. He is disciplined both spiritually and physically, so his body or mind doesn't have mastery over him. He is patient, kind, and gentle. He is graceful and merciful. He has a heart for God's people. If he doesn't, then he'll rule over them instead of leading alongside them.

If you aspire to ministry, know that there is more to being a minister than what is seen in the public arena. The heart and soul of the called one must be a reflection of the very heart of God. Seek to become the kind of person who is worthy of the responsibility of ministry. Not just someone who sees ministry as something to do.

WAITING ON GOD

Waiting is a prerequisite for exaltation, which some would assume to be a higher ranking in ministry. However, true exaltation is the death of your will, your way, and your desires for everything God desires for you. It is your death on the cross—your old life being put to rest—in exchange for a new way of living and a renewed mind. It's one of the most critical periods in the journey of ministry, but it's the toughest for our earthly minds to understand. Our culture is fast-paced. Everything is purposed to be quick, fast, and in a hurry. We live in a world where food must be fast, grits must be instant, plates must be microwaved, the internet must be at top speeds, and transportation must be at the speed of a bullet. We want to get everything quickly, be everywhere faster, and have anything without waiting. This fast-paced mindset has caused us to discount the importance of waiting. You might roll your eyes because you want to get moving and feel you do not have the luxury of waiting. However, life has taught me that waiting on the Lord is more valuable than anything else.

First, we must consider what it means to wait on the Lord.

Second, we must consider Who we are waiting on.

Third, we must consider what we are waiting for.

Fourth, we must examine the life of David as he waited to assume the kingship after being anointed by God.

What does it mean to wait on the Lord? I want to paint a picture for you in hopes that it can provide clarity on this issue. Some would assume waiting means they will do nothing. Some would argue that it means they should continue doing what they're already doing without adding anything extra. Both definitions have some truth in them; however, they do not fully encompass what it means to wait on the Lord.

The phrase "wait on the Lord" makes most people uncomfortable because it challenges their pride. It endangers their sense of control. Due to our fast-paced society, we've been conditioned to think that what doesn't come fast must be abandoned. Because we don't see it when we want it, we try to work harder for what we desire in order to see it come quicker. Unfortunately, there's a reason why what we desire isn't something we really need at that particular time. God is so wise in all He does, and He has good reasons for why we should wait for His provision and in His timing.

The phrase isn't popular because some assume that God is either mad at them or He doesn't prefer them. If God does not answer our prayers immediately or within the timetable we give Him then we begin to suspect that something must be wrong. We tend to think that maybe He's trying to teach us a lesson. Some assume that they must try to manufacture an answer by trying to manipulate God—as if they could—in order to bring something to pass that they greatly desire. It's like they go to the store, buy the gift they want, wrap it up real nice with a big bow, and put God's name on it as the sender. Some assume they need to give more of their money, more of themselves, more of their time, or more of their devotion to see that the answer comes quickly. Others think that they should just move forward with whatever they were waiting on and hope that God will bless it. And still others will assume they should just do whatever they want to do and hope God will be pleased with it. I'm sure you have probably found yourself in at least one of these different scenarios. What's important is to consider what it means to truly wait on the Lord.

Hebrew is a pictorial language. We can understand a word by thinking about the original action, which helps us to draw a picture of it. We can understand what it means "to wait" by identifying the picture behind the words. Imagine a picture of multiple strands of rope being gathered and twisted together. These strands are being intertwined tightly, so they do not unravel. What we need is a tight rope, which can represent many things like trust, hope, and love. God is in the intertwining. Each step of our journey is another twist of the rope. Through the process of waiting, He is teaching us to trust Him, place our hope in Him, and to remain at rest in His love. He is knitting you together with Him. You are coming on the same accord, and His cords are not thin! His threefold cords are not broken!

Oftentimes what we see is the need—the thing we are asking God for or what we desire for Him to do. We want the need met immediately because we feel like time is running out or it has run out. Our backs are against the wall, we have nowhere else to turn, and we need heavenly intervention. We're at the point that if God doesn't respond with what we have asked for, then we'll be ruined. If He doesn't reveal our purpose, then we won't know where to go.

Because we focus so much on the need, we fail to think about what God is truly doing. Some will ask themselves where God is in their time of need or what He is doing. They might assume He's just looking idly on while they sit in a puddle of tears and are pushed into a cocoon of despair. God is collecting strands and binding them together. We are being bound to Him in this process. This is probably one of the most important processes of your reborn life.

For example, you are praying and asking God to give you purpose. You're hungry to know what He's called you to do. You're fasting for the answer. You lay with your face to the floor every night searching for the answer. You want and need it by any means necessary. But it seems like God is silent. You do everything within your power not to become angry and frustrated, especially when it seems like of the rest of your family and friends are excelling in their lives. It feels like you're all alone, and no one cares. "Where is God!" you ask. "What is He doing?" you question. He's collecting and binding the strands together. You're put into a position where you can learn a valuable lesson while these strands are being bound together. You're learning how to trust Him.

"But Cornelius, how in the world am I learning how to trust Him?" you may find yourself asking. Well, you'll find yourself in a place where you have no other choice but to lean on Him. You can't turn back now. You have to trust Him. You're learning that nothing else matters in the world except yearning for Him. You get to the point where you spend hours praising Him in your closet just to have a few minutes saturated in His glory. You learn that even though you don't have the answer you have Him, and He becomes all you need. You thought the answer was what you needed when you really needed to just be content in Him. You're learning that He is the priority. You're learning to be disciplined in your life. He's teaching you so much while those strands are being bound together.

Most of the time you think it's all about you, but there are multiple things going on behind the scenes that you know nothing about. More people are being impacted through your perceived difficulty than you realize. You thought it was all about you and an answer to your prayer. He's teaching you something much more valuable—the value of seeking Him for who He is and not just for what He can give to you.

This time of waiting is so important as well because it teaches you to get out of thinking that the answer you seek will look the way you think it should. That it will come the way you expect it. You finally sit back and allow God to be God. It's somewhat like what my mother used to tell me when, as a young man, I tried to tell her how to drive. I'd be sitting in the backseat trying to tell her where to turn or how fast to go. She would look in the backseat and remind me that she was the driver. She would quickly tell me to let her drive. That was my cue to be quiet and allow her to do what only she could do—drive.

Pride usually causes us to think we can do better than the one driving, serving, or leading. We assume that the limited information we have in our current position somehow makes us qualified to be in the same position they're in. But we fail to realize that they're looking at a bigger picture while we're focused on a few minor details. From the backseat, I wasn't paying attention to the traffic, the lights, the potential accidents, and everything else going on around me. My view was limited, and my distractions were many.

This is common when you're not in the driver's seat; therefore, I needed to realize my position in the backseat and the limited information I had. I had to stop trying to direct the driver. You must stop doing that as well. If God is truly leading you, then realize that He can see a lot more than you can. He can cause you to avoid potential accidents and construction zones. He knows where He is taking you, so trust Him. Enjoy the ride!

Waiting on God is holding on tight and knowing He is not trying to punish you. He is the Potter forming a masterpiece, the Creator forming a creation, and a Rope Maker weaving delicate strands of a rope together for you to firmly grasp. Consider how beneficial it is to have a strong and sturdy rope to hold on to. You can firmly grasp an intertwined rope, but it's difficult to hold onto a rope that's starting to unravel. And trust me when I say you don't want the rope to unravel. Waiting on Him means the strands are being tightly woven together. So, the longer the wait, the tighter the rope. And the tighter the rope, the greater the need for you to grasp it. Consider that maybe He's preparing you for something so dangerous and so miraculous that you have no other choice but to have a well-woven rope to hold on to. That rope represents your trust in Him as He has tightly woven you together with Him.

We must also consider who we are waiting on. You must realize that you are not waiting on an earthly being. You are not waiting on an answer, a position, or an idea. You stand flatfooted and with your heels dug in the ground because you're waiting on the Holy God. He is the deity that's threading your strands together. Consider who He is. He is not some come-by-lately earthly being that just showed up in the last century. He's not some statue sculpted by man's hands or some idea born from an intellectual. He is not some subject studied in classrooms or an entity that existed after the world was formed.

No, He is the Creator of all creation. He is the Hope of all hope. He formed the galaxies and all the solar systems in the whole universe. He hung the planets in the sky. He placed the stars in the heavens. He placed the Earth close enough to the sun for warmth but far enough that it isn't engulfed by it. He commands the waves of the ocean to cease at the shore. He created creatures with wings to have dominion over the air. He created creatures with fins and gills to have dominion in the depths of the sea. He created man out of the dust of the ground. It was in His likeness that we were fashioned and with His breath that we were given life. It's because of His strength that we don't crumble; because of His faith that we don't give up; because of His wisdom that we are not lost; because of His sight that we are not blind. Can you imagine the One you're waiting on? This is not like you're waiting for a taxi cab or for your meal to come to your table. No!

Consider the works of His hands. He split the sea for the Jews to escape the oppression of the Egyptians. I'm sure they probably suspected that God would possibly build a bridge, but He called them to walk on the floor of the Red Sea. He sent ravens to feed His prophets and saved His anointed from the jaws of lions. He covered His beloved from being engulfed inside the fiery furnace and rescued His chosen. He became flesh to dwell among us, endured earthly temptation, suffered violent persecution, died on the cross to become our sacrifice, became victorious over hell, and redeemed the lost by splitting the veil that once kept us from approaching the Throne of Grace.

This is not some actor on television seeking to portray a god. No, this is the Holy God. It is He who was, is, and always will be. He is the Alpha and Omega. There were none before Him, and there will be none after Him. There's no way you can impeach Him from His throne, and I can guarantee that He will never resign. I'm sure it can be a lot for us to wrap our mind around the awesome God we serve, but I beg of you to consider the One on whom you say you're waiting. Can you not rest in Him?

When you know who He is, rest should be simple. Notice I said it should be simple. Oftentimes we find ourselves warring with being at rest. This type of rest involves being confident and keeping our trust in the Lord. It means we are to maintain our faith and confidence in Him without failing. We lean on Him while fully knowing that He will never fail to support us. Entering His rest is a spiritual act. God's people, faithful believers, are the hardest-working and most productive people you'd ever meet. God has not called any man or woman to be lazy. We rest spiritually in Him and work passionately with our hands. We find rest in Him, so our soul may be refreshed and satisfied.

Let me ask you a serious question that I want you to ponder. Is God worthy to be trusted? Consider the question. I am not asking if you are worthy of being trusted. I didn't ask if God answered your past prayers. Some would assume that God's answering, or lack thereof, would somehow qualify Him for future trust. I didn't ask if the journey of waiting was difficult. I didn't ask how you felt about it. I want you to completely put your feelings aside for a moment. Consider the evidence you read in the past few paragraphs. Consider the proof that's written throughout Scripture. Is God worthy to be trusted? Yes or no?

Based on the evidence, He's more than worthy to be trusted. Therefore, settle it in your heart that you will trust Him despite what it looks like, feels like, or sounds like. Trust Him. He doesn't have to earn your trust now. He's already deserving of it, and He proved it when He redeemed you from the curse of the Law and set you free from the pit of sin. He's entitled to it from the beginning of time when He could've killed all of mankind but spared a few to repopulate the land He created. Just consider the One you're waiting on.

I can understand waiting on the Lord and how stressful that process can be. After dropping out of college, I was in a period of waiting on the Lord. I was learning how to put my trust in Him. He was tightly braiding my strands together. He was fitly joining me to Himself. We were becoming intertwined, but I was growing impatient. I felt like I should be doing more than living back home in my parent's home. I was frustrated and didn't understand why God would lead me to a pit of despair.

I questioned if I even heard from Him. I began to doubt my own existence. I contemplated suicide multiple times. I was so hurt and disenchanted with life. All I had was my Bible, my room, and my closet. I took all my clothes out of it, put a small lamp on the floor, and that became my place to seek Him. I wanted to do more. I felt like I should be on the mission field or something. I just didn't like being stuck in my house studying the Word and praying. I didn't realize it at the time, but God needed me there. I needed to learn to trust Him when my life was not turning out how I desired it.

See, my perspective was limited just like it was in the backseat of my mother's vehicle. My view was limited. You must understand that your view is limited as well. While you might be focused on the promise that you think you deserve or are tired from the journey you're on, you must recognize that the same God that led the redeemed mankind from hell is capable of seeing to it that you get where you're supposed to be when you need to get there! Rest in that truth.

We must also consider what we are waiting for. I sat down with a young man for lunch, and he told me about his journey of faith and how he came to the knowledge of the truth. I was intrigued by his story of triumph and victory. He escaped death more than three times. One of them was when his mother was talked out of getting an abortion by the secretary at the clinic. Another was when he was in a serious car accident. The last time was when he was violently beaten by his stepfather.

His story of trials and tribulations were heartbreaking but encouraging. He began to tell me about his walk of faith. He believes God's mighty hand is on Him. He believes He's been called to preach to a broken world and snatch men from the gates of hell. He was frustrated because he was in a waiting period. I asked him what the most frustrating thing about the waiting period was. He responded by saying, "I don't know what to wait for."

I believe this is a common theme among people who are waiting on the Lord. Many are looking for signs and wonders. Some are looking for certain verses to jump off the pages of the Bible. There are some who are going from conference to conference and event to event to hear the words of a preacher in the hope that God will speak through the preacher to them as they sit in the audience. All in all, it seems like the majority of people are not sure what to look for. Like that young man, they're waiting on something. They don't know if it's going to fall from the sky or be sent to their front door. They just don't know.

Waiting on the Lord is a privilege if you value it as one. A privilege is an opportunity that isn't afforded to everyone. It's one you are given, and it must not be taken for granted. While I do not suggest that not everyone can wait on God, I am saying that many do not understand the value in waiting. They are quick to rush to meet their own demands without considering His direction. You will make a terrible mistake if what you're waiting on is an earthly thing. I've known men and women to wait on buildings, people, and ideas, but their waiting was wasted on the product, not the Creator. They thought they were waiting to finally get in a certain position, but their hope was misplaced. Your reward is not the "Promised Land." It's not earthly prosperity or popularity. Your goal is full and complete trust in the Lord. Mark 8:36 asks a very relevant question: "For what does it profit a man to gain the world, and forfeit his soul?" What good would it be for you to have an earthly position only for the same crowd that applauded you to then turn their backs on you? What good is it for you to finally get the building you've been praying for only to have an earthly storm come through and tear it down within a matter of seconds? What good is it to get all the money you've been asking for only to lose it all when the banks close their doors? What good is it to have the diabetes taken away only to realize that your habits, the ones that caused the issues, have never changed?

You can hope and holler for the things you want as long as you want, but what good does it make? It was his trust in God that caused Elijah to be victorious on top of Mount Carmel. It was trust in God that strengthened a young David to fire a single stone with a slingshot at the giant Goliath. It was trust in God that propelled Noah to continue building the ark before the rain came. It was trust in God that sustained each and every one of His prophets. I'm sure they were glad when their ropes were tightly wound. When the world fades away, and nothing is left to stand on, you'd better hope you have a rope that's tight enough to hold on to. And you'd better hope that the hand on the other end of that rope is from the Lord! Because if it's not God, that's tying you to Himself, then rest assured that the enemy is wrapping his strands around you so he can suffocate you with them. He desires to twist you up in His web of deceit until you are destroyed. Do not take the bait! He'll use all the things of the world that tempt you until they ruin you! Wait on the Lord!

SPIRITUAL MATURITY

First Corinthians 13:11 reads, "When I was a child, I spoke and thought and reasoned as a child. But when I grew up, I put away childish things." Everyone has to grow up. Time does not stop for anyone. We get older, and we gain more experiences daily. We all must start as children with all of the deficiencies and limitations that entails.

Since the beginning of mankind there has not been a man or woman to emerge from his or her mother's womb with a fully matured body and mind. We all must progress and grow. This particular verse highlights the growth process we all go through. When we are children, we think, act, talk, and move like children. However, our thoughts, actions, talking, and movements change as we mature. This maturity process is physical, mental, and spiritual. The body matures over time. Our ability to perceive and understand things mentally also changes. We develop emotionally over the years learning a variety of nuances. And, along with all these, we must grow spiritually.

When we emerge from the womb of grace, that is the time we are saved as spiritual children. We must make every effort to make sure we do not remain that way. There are three stages of spiritual growth I will highlight in this chapter; the *nepios*, or infant/childlike stage;

teknon, or teenage stage, and *huios*, or the stage of sonship and maturity.

SPIRITUAL BABIES

The Greek word for 'child' in 1 Corinthians 13:11 is *nepios*. It means infant, child, or unlearned. It suggests that the person is unlearned and unenlightened. This person is immature, a beginner, or a new convert. They are not fully developed because some things have yet to mature before she or he is able to perform independently. The child is impressionable and easily influenced. They will readily receive what they should have thrown away. Because they cannot properly discern what the best decision is for them, they retain or pick up things that could be harmful or deadly.

When my wife was in the hospital having our children, they gave us special wristbands with my wife's name on them. They were purposed to match our child with us. I know we all like to think our children look exactly like us when they emerge from the womb, but that is not an accurate description of what happens. If we were honest with ourselves, we would admit that they are a little unrecognizable.

When they wheeled my son into the nursery after he was born, I quickly ran over to see him. I pressed my face against the glass that separated us and started to make little noises to a baby I thought was my son. I was there for about ten minutes telling a child that I loved him so much. I showered him with so many words from my heart. Then, the nurse walked up to me and said, "Mr. Lindsey, Logan is over there!" My heart leaped from my chest. I had just spilled my heart to someone else's child. My wife and I laughed about it afterward, but I realized that day that babies could all look the same. They do not mirror the parents in appearance or identity yet! This is true physically, mentally, and spiritually.

A new convert does not mirror the life of Christ. You will not see servanthood and sacrifice like you would in an adult. They are children. As time progresses, their features begin to mirror the parents. In the same way, spiritual children will start to look like the Father in word and deed by the fruit that is produced in them by the Holy Spirit. This fruit will be seen in their speech and in their actions. There is no doubt that my son and I are "twins," but that took time to happen.

Having small children has helped me understand this process. I was a child once, but I do not remember much of my life at that time. Seeing my children up-close has helped me understand the *nepios* stage of spiritual growth. My children are very impressionable. My wife and I have to constantly make sure we watch what they are watching, reading, who they are around, or what they are putting in their mouths. I cannot count the number of times I have snatched something from my children that was harmful. They cried because they wanted it, but I had to take it because they were about to put the harmful product in their mouth. It could have been deadly. Those in this stage need constant supervision. Like children, when they are quiet, you must be concerned because anyone with a lot of curiosity but little self-control and discernment is a danger to self and others.

My son is the oldest of our two children, so I have definitely learned a great deal fathering him. There are times when I am amazed at how much he thinks he knows and how much he thinks I do not. He has told me countless times that he knows what he is doing. A few of those times he has come back and asked for help after realizing he could not do what he desired to do alone. I am amazed at what he thinks he can actually do by himself, but that is one of the many attributes of the spiritual child. She or he will go through life trying to do things for himself or herself without asking for help. And the result is usually disastrous!

My son wanted a bag of skittles that were on the top of the table. My wife offered to grab them for him. He just needed to wait until she was finished with what she was doing. I'm not sure if he realized it, or if he cared, but my wife and I had other food on the table. My son was impatient—which is another trait of spiritual infancy—and he pushed his small stool to the table. He climbed as high as he could, and he reached as far as he could with his little arms. The candy was in the middle of the table, so there was no way he was going to reach it. However, he was determined, which can be a very good trait in this stage.

He proceeded to climb on top of the table to retrieve the candy. As he lifted his other leg onto the tabletop, he and the table tipped over, and all the food that was on it went crashing to the floor! My wife and I were upset, but we had to remember that he was a child. He was only doing what children do. They explore and try to do things on their own instead of waiting for assistance.

One of the dangers of those in this stage is that they can be easily manipulated. That is in large part because there is a natural conceitedness born out a desire for independence. This is why we are encouraged in 1 Timothy 3:6 to not allow new believers to be elders. They cannot hold a high position in the church because they are unskilled and not ready for the role. Their conceit comes from what they think they know.

Have you ever met someone who knew a lot, but did not really understand anything? They are knowledgeable about many things but they do not understand or have a concept of what they know. They are walking encyclopedias without a true understanding of what they have learned. These are the people who have read or heard many scriptures but do not understand enough to articulate them well contextually.

One example that really sticks out to me is when I hear someone use the first part of Matthew 7:1 as their reasoning for allowing those in continuous sin remain in their ways. They shout out, "DO NOT JUDGE OTHERS!" Or, some say, "DO NOT JUDGE ME!" I am quick to let them know that judgment is not a bad thing. We learn from John 3:19 that the judgment has already come. Jesus did not come to judge the world, but to save it. He came because there was already a verdict, and He is the only one who can provide a way of escape from the ruling. We are all judging and passing judgment on others. Preaching has a sense of judgment in it because we are simply sharing the judgment with others. We are giving them the verdict while using the scripture as evidence to back up our claim in the court of public opinion. Therefore, the verse really speaks about being hypocritical in our assessment of others, not denying someone the right to preach the truth just because you do not want to hear it. It is examples like this one that shows the immaturity in the spiritual child. The great thing is that they can learn, but they must be willing to be taught.

Another important characteristic of the spiritual child is his or her inability to walk or talk with maturity. We did not emerge from our mother's womb saying full sentences and walking to the bathroom. We depended on our guardians for everything. We had no other choice but to trust our parents in hopes that they would meet our needs and supply our wants. A great characteristic of the spiritual child is the concept of childlike faith, which is simply believing God at His word like a child would his or her parent. I know that if I tell my son that I am taking him to get a game, he does not forget it. He will ask me over and over again when we are leaving to go to the store. He believes we are going, and he is relentless until he gets what he is hoping for. But the child has to learn that trust.

In the same way, the child must learn how to speak and walk correctly. It is foolish to expect a new convert to immediately know everything there is to know about our Christian faith. He was just born! And there is a lot he needs to learn. It is also foolish to expect her to be able to walk by faith like Abraham or Noah. The spiritually immature are babies. Mirroring their physical limitations, they must be taken everywhere for a season until they are able to get to their destinations independently. Even so, the child must be watched to make sure she or he does not do something that could result in hurt, harm, or danger. I have learned over the years that it is foolish to expect new converts to suddenly have bold faith that has not been tested, tried, and proven sure. They need time to grow.

One major attribute of the spiritual baby is their attitude when they are told 'no.' When you tell the *nepios* 'no,' she or he cries. When I tell my children no, they usually throw a temper tantrum. This is because they want what they want even though what they want is not good for them. Crying, screaming, rolling on the floor, and making a spectacle of themselves is the only way, they assume, they can get what they want when they want it. And sometimes it works, especially with our children. My wife and I will give in to quiet them. This can be harmful because it teaches the child that crying and screaming is an effective form of communicating their desires and needs. If we do not talk it out and help our children process their emotions, they will spend a good part of their lives manipulating others to get what they want with tears or any other emotionally manipulative method. Because of this emotional instability, it is dangerous to place the word of God in his or her hand. Ephesians 6:17 refers to the word of God as the Sword of the Spirit. It is a double-edged sword that cuts deep down. No wise parent would put a double-edged sword in the hands of an emotionally unstable child without proper supervision. Allowing him to handle such a sharp object can be deadly and dangerous. Think about the number of people around the world who have been seriously wounded by a spiritual baby who used the word of God like a dagger to inflict pain. It is important the spiritual baby matures, and that this maturity can be seen in how he chooses to submit to authority for instruction and guidance, his willingness to accept responsibility for decisions, his desire to be accountable for his actions, and his willingness to be disciplined when in error. These attributes mean the child is moving to the next stage of growth.

SPIRITUAL TEENAGERS

The spiritual teenager mirrors almost every teenager walking the earth right now. You might be reading this book as a teenager, so you will understand some of the attributes. If you are older, then you will see how you used to be. Ultimately, this stage is an important one. Spiritual children are not recognizable in identity or action, but spiritual teenagers are beginning to show some resemblance to the influential adults in their lives. They are starting to look more and more like the Father and their actions mirror His words, which means they are obedient to what He tells them to do.

However, just because they start to look like the Father does not mean they do not need to be trained. Those who are physically teenagers need training if they are to run the Father's business. The same is true spiritually. If you are going to operate in God's calling for your life, then you must be trained. He will not allow a novice to run His business! No wise father would do that. In fact, Jesus showed us this example. He knew when His time would come to "run the Father's business."

Luke 3:23 tells us that He was 30 years old when He started His ministry. There was training that had to be done first. Luke 2 tells us that Jesus was found in the Temple after Mary and Joseph noticed He was missing. He was there learning and being trained. Prayer, which was an act He faithfully performed, was a big part of His training. There was a lot He needed to learn, and He shows us the process of being trained and groomed for ministry.

Sadly, many spiritual teenagers feel they know everything. I thought I knew everything as a teenager. I felt like my mother and father did not know anything at all! From the ages of 13 to 19, I felt like my parents were amateurs. It wasn't until I got older and had more responsibility that I realized I did not know as much as I thought I did. Pride is a huge obstruction for spiritual teenagers. They think having lived, experienced, and learned some things over the years somehow gives them the right to assume the role of know-it-all. But, like me, they soon find out that they do not know everything. Life has a way of humbling you. I know that from experience.

There can be many instances where the spiritual teenager does not delight in discipline, responsibility, or accountability. For example, he will ask for a car when he gets his license. He is willing to drive it, get it washed, and run a few errands in it, but that is where he draws the line. He expects for his parents to give him gas money, change his tires, or make sure his oil is changed. The problem is that it is his car. He asked for it. He is showing some signs of responsibility with it, but he will not accept it in full. When he runs out of gas, his father chooses not to take him anywhere. He allows him to solve the problem for himself. The teen gets angry with his dad because he does not like the discipline! He does not want to be accountable for his actions, and he refuses to take full responsibility. Even in all of this, he does not see how he is wrong.

It is usually with this kind of attitude and during this stage that people leave churches. They jump from church to church, marriage to marriage, school to school, or house to house every time they are disappointed, disciplined, or held responsible for their actions. They do not like it, so they run. And this is what spiritual teenagers do; they run! This is why you see so many teenage runaways. Children are kidnapped; teenagers run! They have full use of their legs, so they choose to use them. They keep running until they realize that the situations in which they find themselves are not the problem. Rather, the issues are within them, which is their refusal to take full responsibility, unwillingness to be disciplined, lack of desire to be taught, submissive, and accountable. They can keep running trying to find something new, but the old them is going to keep showing up!

Some other characteristics of the spiritual teenager is a desire to argue over silly things, which is a symptom of thinking they know everything. Because they assume they know everything, and do not do anything wrong, they are willing to expose everyone except themselves. They know what is right, and everyone else is wrong. They are the voices in the crowd that is quick to call a woman a 'Jezebel' or refer to a preacher as a 'false prophet.' They do not need solid evidence presented to them in their "courtroom of justice" to pass a verdict. But they demand you show full proof of why they are guilty of anything.

The biblical characters that personify these words are the Pharisees and Sadducees. These Jewish groups were strict observers of tradition and the written law. They were very self-righteous, which means they used their actions as evidence of their redemption. They lacked grace and mercy. Jesus was in constant conflict with both parties. They held strong to their beliefs even though they were wrong. Although rebuked, they did not listen or change. They were accountable to no one, but themselves. And they were not willing to be taught.

Spiritual teenagers fill our churches today. Many get stuck in this stage. They do not reach the maturation of the faith, which includes wisdom, responsibility, accountability, submission, service, love, and sacrifice. Nevertheless, this group can have some great qualities. They can be some of your most energetic people in the church. Unfortunately, you cannot fully rely on them. They can be very zealous to learn, but their zeal can lead to an over accumulation of the wrong information. Because of the wrong information, they will start providing recommendations that are not biblical. Some will use it to defend their perverse actions. Others will share what they have heard without a full understanding of it. Their desire to read God's words, or the words man have written about Him, becomes more important than spending time with Him to get to know Him—which can be summed up in a strong, continuous prayer time.

Finally, one of the most difficult things the spiritual teenager has to realize is that he is not ready to take over the family business. Imagine "looking" like your father, but still not ready to run anything. They desire the irresponsibility and immaturity of childhood with the freedom and resources of adulthood, but you cannot have it both ways. They have the height, strength, and intellectual capability of an adult, but lack the permission and experience to venture out on their own. It is like feeling trapped in a waiting room. You sit there awaiting your turn in line to experience the freedom and resources of adulthood!

It was that feeling you had when you wanted your first car. You desired the freedom to drive when you wanted and the resource of having a car. But, you did not delight in the responsibility of paying for it or being mature enough to take care of it. All you wanted was a car. The object was the symbol of everything you thought you wanted. But, you couldn't see beyond it.

Patience and self-control will be two of the fruits that are developed at this stage. When the spiritual teenager begins to show signs of accepting full responsibility, acknowledging his or her wrongdoings, being willing to be accountable, refusing to run from being taught and disciplined, and honoring authority, these are clear signs that they are in preparation for the next stage.

SPIRITUAL ADULT

Being mature does not mean you never make mistakes or are without flaws. However, it does mean you refuse to allow those flaws to go unnoticed. You are willing to confront and deal with them. You no longer cry and whine like the child or run away like the teenager. You are willing to stay and accept the discipline because you know it is for your good. You are willing to remain married even though you are going through a rough season. You are willing to continue pastoring the church God told you to plant because you realize He called you to do it. God's calling was not based on the number of people who showed up for service!

You accept responsibility. You do not pass the blame to someone else. You are willing to accept what you have done and the consequences. You also accept the responsibility of your call. Unlike the child (who cries because she or he doesn't want it) and the teenager (who runs from it), you are willing to remain obedient no matter the situation or circumstance. Nothing can remove your hand from the plow. You are like the apostle Paul. You are confident and sure in what you are called to do, and you refuse to allow anyone to change it.

Because your faith has been tested and proven, you trust God at His word. You freely ask Him questions without questioning Him. The difference between the two should not be cast aside as insignificant. When you ask a question, it means you desire information. But questioning means you doubt the information you are receiving, or you do not trust the vessel giving it to you. Because you are cemented in the truth and no longer waver in your faith, you are able to trust God enough not to question His ways or plans. You have endured enough to know that He is with you every step of the way. You have experience after experience to prove it.

You are empathetic, which means you willingly place yourself in another's situation. You feel how they feel. Children can be very selfish—only desiring things for themselves—and teenagers can be apathetic. The adult is willing to be selfless and loving. At this stage, you are mirroring the Father in image and actions.

The child is maturing in his looks and actions. The teenager has a resemblance of the Father, but is not matured yet. He has some actions, but they are not fully developed. He is showing signs that he can preach, but most of it is charisma, not a mature, loving, and skilled exposition of the word of God for the edification of the Body. In fact, the teenager will get angry when anyone says she or he resembles his or her parents. But, the spiritual adult takes it as a compliment. This is because he is fully aware and now understands why his parents made many of their decisions. He may not agree with them, but maturity causes him to at least respect them. You may not agree or like what God chooses to do, but you learn to respect it anyway without questioning His motives or actions. And with respect comes adoration. So, being told he looks and acts like his father is not a bad thing or something to be feared.

Finally, spiritual adults acknowledge their need for help. They are dependent on the Holy Spirit each and every day. They consider Him in all their ways. They have experienced the teenage years of going in their own direction, and they are done with it. They are submitted now, and they know it is the safest place for them to be.

The journey from a spiritual child to a mature adult cannot be cheated. Everyone will pass through every stage. It will be frustrating, but that is the process. Instead of fighting it so much try to learn what God is teaching you in each one. The longer it takes for you to learn the lesson, the longer you will be at the stage, longing for the next one, but seeing it escape your grasp. Don't waste the stage you are in.

OVERCOMING INSECURITIES

I was very insecure for most of my childhood. I was the chubby kid who was not very good at sports. I did not come from wealth neither did I have many friends. In fact, my closest and only friend for many years was my cousin. When I compared myself to my peers, I always concluded that I was inferior. I started to believe that I did not look the best, dress the best, or have the best. I had another big problem that I felt would hinder me for the rest of my life—I stuttered!

I was so insecure about my stutter that I would remain silent so others would not make fun of me. I felt like my speech impediment meant I was handicapped in some way, so I would shy away from doing anything that brought me any attention. I refused to speak publicly. I felt like my command of English was not all that great. I did not feel smart or adequate. Growing up with these self-identified inadequacies led me to believe that God could not use me for His will. I would question anyone who prophesied anything about me. I mean, how could God possibly use someone who had, what I felt, was a disqualifying handicap? It made absolutely no sense at all to me. Then, I realized that I did not truly know God. Here's why.

There is a very familiar story in scripture that I feel mirrors my own in many ways. Moses faced his own insecurities, and like me, he told God what He couldn't do instead of believing what God could do through him. Exodus 4:10-17 reads,

> But Moses pleaded with the Lord, 'O Lord, I'm not very good with words. I never have been, and I'm not now, even though you have spoken to me. I get tongue-tied, and my words get tangled.' Then the Lord asked Moses, 'Who makes a person's mouth? Who decides whether people speak or do not speak, hear or do not hear, see or do not see? Is it not I, the Lord? Now go! I will be with you as you speak, and I will instruct you in what to say.' But Moses again pleaded, 'Lord, please! Send anyone else.' Then the Lord become angry with Moses. 'All right,' he said. 'What about your brother, Aaron the Levite? I know he speaks well. And look! He is on his way to meet you now. He will be delighted to see you. Talk to him, and put the words in his mouth. I will be with both of you as you speak, and I will instruct you both in what to do. Aaron will be your spokesman to the people. He will be your mouthpiece, and you will stand in the place of God for him, telling him what to say. And take your shepherd's staff with you, and use it to perform the miraculous I have shown you.

I know that was a lot, but it is very important for you to read these verses to see with clarity the importance of what this chapter is all about.

It is crucial for you to realize that the verses you just read were about Moses. He is one of the most significant characters of our Christian faith. He is most notably famous for leading the Israelites out of their bondage in Egypt. Have you ever heard the story where the sea split and a road was made for God's people to walk through without sinking or drowning? Well, that story's central character is Moses! His acts of faith and obedience are still spoken about across the world.

I want you to notice that before the miraculous signs took place and the Israelites were set free, he struggled with overcoming his own insecurities. He had not stood in front of Pharaoh yet! Moses' toughest opponent, like yours and mine, was himself. The fear of becoming more than what you already are is very real. It is as real as the fear of becoming more than what you're surrounded by. We become comfortable with our lives as we live them, and anything that attempts to disrupt that comfort is a threat. I have sat with many people who have feared becoming and doing more because they were afraid they would not be able to handle it. They did not think they had enough or were enough to do all they were called to do and be all they were called to be.

One young man's story comes to mind. He was born and raised in the projects by his grandmother. His mother and father were both imprisoned and his cousins were either gang-affiliated, or they had died from gun violence. His only friend was shot down while riding his bicycle home from school in what was described as an accidental shooting. He did not attend the best school, which meant he did not have the best education. He told me how many of his teachers did not care; therefore, they did not try to go above and beyond to reach the students.

In spite of these difficulties, he was given an opportunity to be mentored by an influential doctor in the city. He was able to shadow him for almost two years. At his graduation, the doctor gave him a scholarship to attend a college where he had applied and was accepted. The young man was overwhelmed at the possibility of escaping his poverty-stricken surroundings. He was accepted into both an Ivy League and a community college. The community college was not too far from where he grew up. After a couple of weeks of deliberation, he decided to attend the community college.

His mentor met him for lunch to inquire as to why he chose the community college over the Ivy League institution. His reasoning was because he did not want to leave his surroundings. He did not want to leave his friends behind or journey too far from where he grew up. He wanted to stay close to what he knew and who he knew. And the thought of leaving the state was more than he could handle. Although disappointed, the mentor honored his agreement and gave the young man the scholarship to attend the community college. Unfortunately, he did not stay in college long. He started skipping classes to hang out with people he knew at home. He did not feel challenged, so he did not give his best. It was an unfortunate situation. To this date, the young man still has not escaped his surroundings to achieve his best.

The bondage of people's perception is powerful! It can keep you from reaching your fullest potential. It snatches you back whenever you attempt to move forward. What's heartbreaking is when the people you love play a part in trying to keep you mediocre by pulling you back to where you were. Making it so you do not advance ahead of them. The very thought of you moving ahead threatens them and their comfort. To see you driving away highlights their position and immobility. They could either encourage you on your journey or get in a car and follow you, but many do not do that. Their insecurity and the spotlight placed on their position because of your success makes them bitter towards you. They see your progress as unnecessary and threatening. You must fight back by not giving in to the demands of comfort and by not getting caught in their bondage. You cannot afford to remain the same place you have been just because you are too afraid to stand up against your community; to challenge those around you who desire to keep you stagnant. Always remember that the most effective leader is the individual who can free himself from the bondage of other people's perceptions and opinions. Then, and only then, will he be free enough to serve them. Your community, family, and friends need you to excel and move forward with what God is calling you. Only then will you be able to become an instrument in God's hand so they can one day benefit from your obedience. No, they may not like it in the beginning, but that is okay. There are times when you must rock the boat to have smooth sailing. It is fine.

Your insecurities cannot be the reason you remain immobile. Being in bondage to them too long will cause you to grow a dependency on them. You will begin to tell God what He cannot do based on whatever deficiency you think you have to accomplish His mission. Like Moses, you'll tell God what you lack as if He doesn't already know it. "Oh Lord, I'm not very good with words." Here's a question to ponder; why worry about what you don't know or don't have when you're being led by the One who has it all?

James 1:5 reassures us that God gives wisdom to those who ask of Him. And, He gives it liberally. Moses was insecure about his speech. I'm sure there are some things you are insecure about as well. It could be that you don't think you are tall enough, strong enough, smart enough, preacher enough, or beautiful enough. You cannot allow whatever you think you don't have to stop you from presenting yourself to God so He can fill you. Just remember that He can make you enough. He will put the words in your mouth as He did for Jeremiah. You must overcome the fear and step outside of your insecurities. Fear leads to inactivity, and you overcome it with action. Be bold. Be courageous. Refuse to live in fear.

Years ago, I started a job that would be very influential to my journey. I learned so much from it even though it did not begin like I thought it would. In the first couple of days, I was told that I wouldn't be able to finish the job. I was called "worthless," and referred to as a "nobody." The words cut deep, as most hurtful words do. I've learned over the years that the people you love the most and are around can do the most damage to your soul. I spent many of those days wounded. I knew I had to snap out of my sorrow, and the only way I knew to go about it was self-affirmation. I stood in front of my bathroom mirror and said to myself, "You are somebody!" I kept saying it until I believed it!

Could you believe that I stood in front of that mirror talking to myself for almost two hours? It took that long for me to empty myself of the words spoken over me so I could finally accept and believe what I knew God believed about me. To the rest of world, I'm fine with being a nobody, but to God—I'm worth dying for! And you are, too! You are somebody, and none of your insecurities can stop you from doing what God has called you to do and becoming all He has called you to become.

TRAINING AND PREPARATION

George Foreman, who is arguably one of the greatest boxers to ever live, won the IBF and WBA boxing titles twenty years and six days after he lost the undisputed heavyweight championship to Muhammad Ali. I could only imagine his rigorous training schedule to achieve it. Michael Jordan, a name that is synonymous with great basketball, trained as hard off the court as he played on the court. If we tried writing a list of great performers and athletes, it would be more than a mile long. What sets them apart from everyone else is a very small list of attributes. However, there's one key attribute that stands out and is shared by most, if not all of them—their willingness to train and prepare.

I played football for two years while in middle school. Was I any good? Absolutely not! It was not because I wasn't capable of being the best. I was not good because I refused to train. I did not want to endure the tough, grueling schedule like everyone else to become the best nose guard on the field. I often practiced poorly. I would cheat and cut corners to get out of practicing. I did not run at my highest speed. I basically stopped caring. I would attribute my lethargic attitude to not really wanting to play football, but I couldn't argue with the fact that I would never know how great of a football player I could have been because I refused to train or give it my all.

I had this same attitude when it came to playing basketball, baseball, and golf. It wasn't until I got serious about working out that I realized the importance of proper training. I realized this quickly because poor form and a lax attitude in the gym could get you seriously injured or even killed. It was my first trainer who convinced me of the importance of preparation. He taught me some important concepts that I believe helped shape my current mentality. He taught me that preparation begins before you arrive. You must give it your all and not assume that certain kinds of training can't prepare you for another part of your journey. Let's analyze this a little further.

I will never forget my first college-level exam. I was a freshman on the campus of the University of Georgia. The class was an introduction to Political Science. This worked well for me because I had in mind to be a political science and international relations double major. I walked into the classroom fully confident in my ability to pass the test with nothing less than a B. My confidence was far too optimistic seeing that I had not fully prepared in the days or weeks beforehand.

I saw many of my classmates in the library studying daily for the exam. They formed study groups and came up with unique ways to remember the material. I was overly confident in my ability without just cause. My only reasoning was that I enjoyed politics and government. I felt like my love for something would trump my need to train in it. Boy, I was wrong! I walked into the classroom that day, sat down in front of the exam, and I started to sweat bullets. This is because one of the scariest days of your life is the day you realize you failed to properly train for something that you had every opportunity to prepare for. The material wasn't new. I just failed to prepare myself. I got my exam back, and I surprisingly did better than I expected. I made a 42, which was a big, fat F, but it was one of the highest scores in the class. My initial thought was: "I wonder how well I could have done had I studied and prepared." I was way beyond that though. I could only think about what hadn't happened, and this event became a learning opportunity for the next time. I assumed my love for the subject would be enough to get a high—if not perfect—score on the exam, but I was wrong. I was going after what I had not worked for, and I was expecting what I did not deserve.

I used to envy the star football player on our junior varsity football team. He was just so good. I attributed how good he was to talent. I wouldn't dare take anything away from him. He was talented. He had some the quickest feet of any player on the field. He excelled at practices and scored during the games. Trust me when I say that his gloating matched his ability. I envied him, but I didn't realize his training schedule. Although he was playing junior varsity football, he trained like a professional player. He was up early working on his footwork. He was disciplined with his eating and resting. He watched games of some of the greatest to get better and gain insight on how to improve his skill. He ate, slept, and drank football. He loved it, and he put his all into it. Nothing could deter him from it. He limited his social interactions with certain crowds to lessen the temptation to get off his schedule.

While waiting for our parents to pick us up from practice one day, he told me how tough his training schedule was. I really wasn't shocked, seeing that his performance matched his preparation! He told me how he had not gone to the movies in over a year since starting to train. He did not have many friends because he could not attend many social outings. He could not go to the parties because many of them started either at or after his bedtime. He had to be in bed early so he could wake up early to train. He had to study, which was not optional because his father refused to allow football to get in the way of his education. He only ate certain foods on certain days, and he had a personal coach to teach him along the way. All in all, he was preparing for what was to come, not for the position he was in.

Consider your journey with God. He's preparing you for what's to come, not for where you are right now. He is preparing you for the obstacles ahead, not for the barriers you're facing right now. He is doing a new work in you that is utterly transformational. And, yes, preparation and training are a big part of that work. This is because the man or woman you are right now is not fit to go into the place He is sending you. There is more you need to know, more you need to believe, and more you must trust Him with. He's building something in you that is completely amazing, but it takes work. And many people do not like work.

Some time ago, I sat with a young man, and we talked about entrepreneurship, business models, financial projections, and trends. It was a great conversation. He looked at me and said, "I am hoping that God gives me what I'm asking for." I looked at him and said, "Brother, God gives shovels." He looked bewildered. "A shovel! Why would He give me a shovel!" I responded, "To dig a ditch."

Too often we are hoping for God to give us the ditch filled with silver and gold. We want to see provision, and we desire to touch the promise. It does not happen that way. You will be trained for your assignment, and proper training is necessary for promotion. You will not be able to escape it because God's hand is on you. You're going to have to dig the ditch in order to enjoy the water God uses to fill it.

I am a firm believer in physical training. I work out daily in some way. My wife jokes that I am always working out. It is nothing to see me on the floor doing push-ups at awkward times of the day. Some would say it is an addiction. I like to think it is a heartfelt desire to maintain my temple. I want it to be in the best shape possible. I work hard at monitoring the food I eat so I am not disqualified from this race due to a poor diet. I joke around with my pastor-friends that it's impossible for me to go to and fro on the entire earth preaching the Gospel if I am stuck in a hospital bed with tubes up my nose and needles in my arm because I refused to take care of the body God gave me.

Some people take 1 Timothy 4:8 out of context. It reads "for bodily discipline is only of little profit, but godliness is profitable for all things, since it holds promise for the present life and also for the life to come." I had someone use that verse to rebuke me for encouraging others to train physically. Notice that the verse says it is of little profit. It does not say it has no profit at all. In comparison to godliness, it is not as important; however, it is still important. Apostle Paul is assigning a greater value to godliness over physical training. Nothing is wrong with that. The problem comes when you dismiss physical training altogether. Do you honestly believe God would desire for you to neglect your body, which is His temple? Do you honestly think He desires for you to fill yourself with contaminated and poisonous foods? I don't think so at all.

Most of us are eating ourselves into a grave! We've become sluggish as a society and as a people, and that shouldn't be. It is sad when church-goers, preachers—self-professing Christians—aren't disciplined in their eating and training. You must realize that God's hand is on you. That means that He has chosen you as one of His own! You are His disciple; therefore, you must be disciplined! In fact, a true disciple is disciplined. Fasting should not be difficult for you. The reason many in the church find it so hard is because of the foods we eat. Going three days without certain foods is difficult because our body goes through withdrawals. It's like we are drug addicts. Sugar calls our name from morning to night. We eat candy and drink sugary drinks throughout the day. We eat greasy foods and pack our stomach full of yeast. Then, we wonder why we are too tired to go soul winning. No, it's not the devil that's holding you back right now. It's the food!

My wife and I are big on healthy habits and physical training. We had a couple of people over at our home one night, and we were asked why we cared so much about what other people ate. We care because it affects you, and whatever affects you can change you. Some people are addicted to food. It has become an idol to them. How can you cast out demons if you cannot overcome the temptation to eat a donut? Have you considered this truth? I would highly recommend that you begin a training schedule that requires a decent amount of working out daily. I also recommend setting up a nutrition plan that targets what you are eating and puts you on the right track. You have to get rid of all the salty foods and sugary snacks. These things are killing you slowly. They are dis-easing the body, and you may not see it now, but the diagnosed disease is on the way.

With so much already against you, don't allow for another thing to be your unwillingness to prepare for what's to come and train for where you are going.

DISCERNMENT IS PARAMOUNT

Discernment is the ability to judge well. It is a gift granted by the Holy Spirit. For this reason, it is one of the most important foundational gifts for the man or woman who's touched by God. He enables the chosen to decide between truth and error, right and wrong. First Thessalonians 5:21-22 makes it clear that Christians must be discerning. We are to examine everything carefully so we can hold to what is good and abstain from evil.

Unfortunately, many do not discern well. This is an area where many stumble. Their inability to examine everything around them prompts them to make decisions that are costly and even dangerous. We would avoid many pitfalls if we'd only take the time to consider the situation and circumstances before making a decision.

God's Word gives us the needed information to discern accurately. Sadly, many do not know and refuse to study God's Word to know how to discern properly. Based on 2 Peter 1:3, God has given us everything we need pertaining to life and godliness. We have it through His Word and the leading and guidance of the Holy Spirit. I strongly believe and counsel that every believer should make it their priority to spend an adequate amount of time in prayer. I do not like to bind my prayer time to a law. In other words, I never make it a set time every time. Each day is different, so I confront each day as its own. I know what is adequate for me because I am satisfied. As a matter of fact, it is like sitting at the table to eat. After you have been filled, it is time to get up. But it is important that you are sensitive to your body to ensure you've received the necessary nutrients.

Years ago, I felt condemned if I did not spend at least an hour in prayer. I felt like God hated me, and I tried to transfer that condemnation on others. Now I practice a consistent reliance on God throughout the day. That means I do not wait until a set time to spend my time with Him. Instead, I consider Him throughout my day through singing of hymns while driving, listening to sermons while working out, or reading my devotionals while sitting around the house. Your 'adequate time' could be two hours a day. Someone else's could be a good devotional after your morning run and before breakfast. It can differ according to the person, but it is important to have it.

The communication we practice with God enables us to know Him more intimately. In fact, intimacy with God is indispensable. To know we have the opportunity to read the Word and to know the Inspirer—who is God—of the word is priceless. To avoid being tossed to and fro and being carried away by false doctrines, worldly philosophies, and New Age idealism, we must study God's Word and spend time with Him. It is incumbent on every believer to understand this principle.

One key aspect of discernment is the ability to carefully identify the people in your village. Who you allow around you and who you choose to listen to is important. You can be easily swayed or choose to quit because of the words you accept from the people around you. Make no mistake about it, bad company will corrupt good character (1 Corinthians 15:33). When God's hand is on you, He will surround you with the right people who are saying the right things to help you reach the right destination. Please understand that the enemy will send the wrong people around you to cause confusion and anger. I know this is true because I have seen it happen in my life many times. There have been several people God has sent into my life to help in some way or another, but there have also been many people sent from the evil one to cause confusion and bring depression. They both have a purpose. It is through discernment that I am able to find out exactly who's who.

One key passage that helps us know the false from the real is found in Luke 6:43-45. It reads:

> A good tree can't produce bad fruit, and a bad tree can't produce good fruit. A tree is identified by its fruit. Figs are never gathered from thorn bushes, and grapes are not picked from bramble bushes. A good person produces good things from the treasury of a good heart, and an evil person produces evil things from the treasury of an evil heart. What you say flow from what is in your heart.

We can gather one very important concept from this passage: a tree is known by its fruit.

There's an old saying that you will never know a man is a fool until he opens his mouth and removes all doubt. You would not have known what was in the man until he revealed it in his speech. Through communication, he revealed his fruit. There is another saying: When someone shows you their true colors—believe them! They are exposing themselves for you to see. Oftentimes, we desire to ignore what people show us. We would rather hope that what we see is not real. Incidentally, we ignore the fruit that openly hangs before us.

Consider if there is a tree filled with oranges. It would be safe to say that it is an orange tree, right? Absolutely! Well, what if we put a sign in front of the tree that reads: "APPLE TREE"? Wouldn't that be misleading? Absolutely! Why? Because the fruit on the tree doesn't match the sign, and yes, they must match. The same is true for self-professing believers. It is absolutely wrong to refer to yourself as a Christian without bearing the fruit of one. If the Holy Spirit truly inhabits us, then we will show fruit. Based on Galatians 5:22-23a, "But the Holy Spirit produces this kind of fruit in our lives: love, joy, peace, patience, kindness, goodness, faithfulness, gentleness, and self-control." If we are truly connected to the True Vine, who is Jesus Christ, then we should produce the fruit of the Spirit. It is that simple. You never have to question if someone has truly been transformed by Christ because you will be able to look at his or her fruit. This is because the fruit will always identify the tree.

There are three very distinct kinds of people that I believe you should carefully observe. How you treat these three people will save you a lot of headache and troubles.

The first set of people you need to discern properly are your confidants. These are the people you can trust with your private matters. You can be "yourself" around them without having to perform. They love you for who you are, and they will be in your life as long as you give them the attention and recognition they rightfully deserve.

The confidant can also be a trusted adviser. Their association with you is based on their undeterred and deeply rooted love for you. Oftentimes, your family can fall in this category. In the beginning stages of ministry, my wife, mother, and sister were the only people who really supported me. I knew God's hand was on me, but it meant so much to have my family there helping, giving, and supporting the vision God planted in me.

It wasn't until after almost three years of ministry that I was honored to meet my best friend. He quickly became a friend I could trust with private matters. He protected me when I was vulnerable and encouraged me when I was down. He, along with my family, served an important role—to encourage me when I felt God had forgotten about me.

Confidants are vital to your journey. You cannot misuse or abuse them. You must honor their presence in your life. You cannot confuse them with those who work with you. Although they are willing to help in whatever capacity you need them, they are not your employees. They are in your life for you.

I sat with an advisor who told me a story of how he lost a confidant. His friend was willing to help in his church in whatever capacity he needed. It just so happened that he really needed help in the media department. His friend did not have much experience in media, but he was willing to oversee the ministry because he loved my advisor. They worked together for almost four years. The media ministry grew until it became one of the greatest ministries at the church. They had more than enough volunteers and skilled craftsmen to create excellent productions. As the church grew, the pastor could pay his friend more money. However, he received word from the Human Resource Director that his best friend had resigned unexpectedly; he couldn't believe it. The pastor contacted his friend and arranged a lunch meeting. They sat down a week later, and he was anxious to ask his friend why he chose to resign. The pastor could not understand the issue. His friend was paid well, over $100,000, and he had the most successful ministry at the church. He was a sought-after leader and was well respected.

They sat down to eat, and the pastor asked his friend the million-dollar question, "What happened?" The best friend looked at the pastor saying, "I don't think you realized why I was at the church. I wasn't there for the money or the acclaim. I was there for you! Unfortunately, you didn't have time for me. That hurt, so it was best for me to leave." The pastor became upset. He couldn't understand why his friend would leave him because of all the things he did for him. But therein lied the problem. The friend was not there because of what the pastor could do for him but remained committed because of what the pastor could do with him. The friend was less motivated by achievement, money, and accolades and more concerned with friendship, comradery, and fellowship.

In 2016, we experienced a very emotionally-charged election cycle. Politics and elections are a dirty business. The primary fight between the Democratic and Republican contenders was downright nasty! The attacks were personal and purposed to inflict great pain long after the election was over. Donald Trump emerged the victor amongst the Republicans; Hillary Clinton, amongst the Democrats. Clinton had a grueling primary battle with Bernie Sanders. They fought tooth and nail for months. Their dislike for one another was apparent; however, they worked hard to put on a good face for the better good of the Democratic Party.

As a lover of politics and elections, I was most intrigued with the relationship between the victor and the loser. Clinton emerged victorious, but it was not without many battle scars to show for it. She had many fresh open wounds that her primary opponent, Trump, was ready to target. Something remarkable and intriguing happened on July 12, 2016. The headlines were: "Bernie Sanders endorses Hillary Clinton." To political novices, I am sure they could not understand how two bitter rivals could join forces after such a nasty primary battle to lead their Party. Some would assume that they buried their animosity for one another long enough to come to the table of brotherhood and settle their issues. That's not what happened. Sanders and Clinton did what many do—and most have done before them—joined together to defeat a common enemy.

Some people will come into your life, and they will resemble trusted friends. This is because they serve to fight alongside you when you need them the most. Although Clinton did not defeat Trump, she needed Sanders' strong, loyal base of voters. Your dedication to defeating the new enemy often creates an illusion that your alliance is faithful. Sanders and Clinton ran for the Democratic nomination and had major ideological differences. They did not see eye-to-eye, and we could see their distaste for one another throughout their primary fight. However, there comes a time when who you are fighting against is more important than who you are fighting with! In this situation, their common enemy, Donald Trump, became a more important target than each other. Therefore, they joined forces with the intent to defeat him.

You must be careful with the second group of people, which I will refer to as— "frenemies." They usually come in your life at a very low, vulnerable moment. You have no other choice but to realize that you truly need them and what they have to offer in defeating your common enemy. However, if you are not careful, you will mistake them for friends. This will lead you to confide in them in your moments of weakness and despair. On the battlefield, you stand back-to-back with your swords drawn. After fighting together all day long, you both become fatigued. You sit down to eat a meal, and in the moment, you let your guard down long enough to divulge information that should only be shared with a trusted confidant. In a place of vulnerability, you shared information that was sensitive and confidential. You thought it was a safe place to share it because your one-time enemy has become what looks like a friend. Unfortunately, after the two of you defeat the common enemy or are defeated by the enemy, the attention is turned back on you. Yes, you will become their next target, and they will begin fighting you where they left off. For this reason, they will use what you told them in private to ruin you in public.

A pastor-friend of mine has a growing church in the Northeast. In addition to cultivating his primary campus, he is working on establishing new campuses. He's a good leader and effective communicator. A year or so ago he got word of a new ordinance the city council wanted to pass that would have limited his ability to open a new campus. The pastor frequented the city council meetings to target the politicians that desired to pass the ordinance. During the process, he noticed that another pastor started joining him at the meetings. However, this was strange to him because he knew the other pastor did not like him. He knew it because the pastor told him to his face many years before. My friend chalked it up to him being jealous of the church's success. Either way, their distaste for one another was apparent.

After one of the meetings, my friend decided to be the bigger man and approach the other pastor. Their conversation was cordial. They even agreed to sit down for lunch to discuss a tactic to kill the ordinance bill. This fight went on for another seven months, but my friend and the other pastor were becoming closer during the process. Well, my friend thought they were becoming closer. After the seven months, the fight was finally won; the ordinance was dead. The next Sunday my friend preached on building a bridge. He preached about the importance of reaching out to those you never thought would be on your side.

After service, he started to receive phone calls from several members of his church. They were irate because of things they heard that he said about them. My friend knew no one could have known what he said unless they overheard his conversations with the other pastor. He refused to believe that the pastor would have betrayed him by leaking all of his personal, private business. That Wednesday before he got on the stage to teach Bible study, he was given a DVD to watch in his office. He popped it in, and there stood the pastor standing behind the pulpit sharing everything my friend told him in private. The pastor used what my friend told him in private to shame him publicly. My friend called me saying, "Cornelius, I don't understand! He was my friend!" I chuckled a little. I talked him into realizing that the pastor was never for him. He did not care about his well-being. The pastor was there for one purpose—to fight their common enemy. After the battle was over, he resumed the battle he put on hold. You must discern who these people are in your life. Giving them too much of yourself can be dangerous. You can often tell who they are based on what they talk about the most. And they usually talk about the enemy.

The third group of people are those who are there for themselves. They aren't for you in any way whatsoever. All they see is a path for them to excel and have more even if it's at your expense.

As a pastor, I've encountered many of these people over the years. At the beginning of my ministry, I took it personally when people left the church. I couldn't understand why they came only to leave. It did not make sense to me. I felt like I gave them everything I had. I paid their groceries, paid mortgages, paid off student loans, fixed cars, and everything else that was asked. I was there when they called and came quickly when they asked. Unfortunately, they left, and some left in great offense. I could not understand it. What could they have been mad about? Then, I finally saw a pattern! Everything was great until I told them "no!" I was the greatest pastor in the world as long as I gave them what they wanted. Consequently, they would leave if I denied them what they wanted. Recognizing that pattern helped me in my journey. I quickly learned to identify those people who only wanted what they wanted. They were not interested in playing on the same team. It was all about them.

Nevertheless, I had to learn how to love them despite their ways. And I had to learn how to encourage them to be team players. I made many mistakes along the way by harshly rebuking them and releasing them from my life. I tried to validate my actions and tell myself that I was right, but I was not. I was just as guilty as they because I refused to gracefully lead them in another direction.

There was a young man who moved to Atlanta to join the church I pastor. I could quickly recognize he was there for himself because all he really talked about was himself. Those who are there for you talk about spending time and getting to know you. They ask how you are doing, and they love to fellowship with you. Those there to help you fight are focused on your common enemy. They talk about the enemy and the plans to defeat him. That's all. Those there for themselves talk a lot about themselves.

This young man talked about himself every opportunity he had. I was the greatest pastor in the world until I would not allow him to preach. He was very upset about it. He left the church less than two months later. I was told that he was given an opportunity to preach at another church. He gladly accepted it. Some would wonder how it could be so easy for him to leave. Well, he was not at the church for me. He was not there to help fight the enemy. He was there for himself. He desired some kind of promotion, and he was willing to do whatever he had to do to get it.

Discerning your associations is very important. Your failure to do so could result in unnecessary hurt and confusion.

PIT TO PRISON TO PALACE

It is my deepest desire and heartfelt prayer that God's Spirit rests on these pages as you read each word. I truly desire for your mind to be opened and that your questions are answered either by something you read or because the Holy Spirit reveals something to you. Being used by God is no light thing; however, grace will meet you on your journey. You are not alone or hopeless. God walks with you every step of the way. You have to trust and believe it. Isaiah 41:10 reads "Don't be afraid, for I am with you. Don't be discouraged, for I am your God. I will strengthen you and help you. I will hold you up with my victorious right hand." That verse has always comforted me when I've felt alone and embarrassed.

There have been many times when I have felt like God abandoned me and left me to suffer. I felt like some of the choices I made caused Him to be upset with me. I've had feelings of condemnation. I've felt so absent of grace without realizing that in the very moment I had the thought of God abandoning me, He was still being merciful and graceful.

I'm reminded of the story of Joseph. It is one of my favorite stories in the Bible. His story is found in the Book of Genesis, chapters 37 through 50. He progressed from a man with a dream to a dream-interpreting slave to the second in command of Egypt. His life is so inspirational because it is filled with a long series of highs and lows—literally and figuratively.

Genesis 37:3 records that Joseph was the favored son of Jacob. His father gave him a garment with long sleeves with stripes of different colors. Joseph's ten older brothers became very jealous because of his special treatment. Throughout your life, you will notice that some will become very jealous of you because of the treatment you are given. They will desire that same treatment, but they will not receive it. This is not because you are any better than they are; it only means that what is for you is only for you. They cannot have what has been laid aside for you. They will not like it, but they will have to learn to deal with it. You must be cautious about how you refer to it. You cannot throw it in their face in conversation or make it seem like you are better or more superior. I've had many situations where things were given to me that I didn't expect. There were other people in line long before I got there, but I was the one who was chosen. There was a time that I was prideful about it, and I had to be humbled.

I attended a very large church for about five years. I liked to sit on the third row every Sunday and Wednesday night. That was one of the few reserved rows. Also, I was there whenever the doors of the church were open. I would drive over two hours to attend Bible study while in college. I felt like I had to be there. There were even times when I did not have the gas money, but I drove anyway. I remember the time I had just enough gas to get me there. I had no clue how I was going to get home. But, I felt like God would meet the need if I moved out in faith. Some would call that foolishness, and I would not disagree with them. However, it was a lesson in trust that

I needed to learn. I had to know that my Father would provide for me as He desired within His will.

As I parked my car in the gravel lot, it shut off before I could turn off the ignition. It was official; I had run out of gas! The good thing was that I made it to church. I had absolutely no money on me at the time. I went in the sanctuary and enjoyed the service. It was an amazing evening. At the close of service, I realized that my car was still out of gas. I was not sure what I was going to do. As I walked in the lobby of the church a woman whom I had never met before in my life came up to me. She said, "God told me to give you this $20! Be blessed." I was overjoyed! Back then, it only took about $13 to fill up my gas tank. I felt like crying. I walked over to my car with the biggest grin on my face. The only problem was that I would have to find a way to get my car to the gas station.

So, I got in my car and put my head against the steering wheel. I was joyful that I had money, but I was so far away from the full provision. That is a sermon by itself. Nonetheless, I sat there and began to research the closest gas stations. I was going to walk there, get gas, and walk back. As I got out of my car, a man approached me. He said, "Son, are you okay?" I responded, "No, I ran out of gas." He looked at me and said, "Well, I guess it's a good thing I brought my truck with me then. I have some gas here. I can put as much as I can in your tank so you can get to the gas station." I felt like falling to my knees and weeping. God provided! I needed that lesson.

I continued going back and forth to church, and that scenario would play out repeatedly. I guess I needed to learn not to drive without gas, but I was willing to abandon my car if I needed to. I've always had a very radical faith. I was intent on driving as far as I could and using the two legs God gave me to journey the rest of the way. I'm thankful that never happened, but I was determined to do it. I wouldn't settle for watching the service online. Technology can help, but it can never replace! Watching a service isn't the same as being there, and I know God wants me to be where He is leading me. If I'm compelled to watch it, then that's a sure sign that I need to be there.

One Sunday at church I was approached by a man I had never seen before. He told me that the pastor wanted my information because he was starting a group where he would mentor men to be church leaders. I was humbled by the acknowledgment. I had a feeling that God's hand was on me, but I wasn't sure. I was not confident about it. It is funny how God will use someone else to confirm what He has already spoken to you. I am forever thankful for the pastor because He was able to see something in me that I did not see in myself at the time. But isn't that what a father is for? He should see the gift in his son and seek to cultivate it. Well, the pastor saw it in me, and he sought to mentor me at a time when I needed it. There were fourteen of us in total, and word got around that I was the last one chosen. That was even more humbling. I sat shoulder to shoulder with men who had known the pastor for decades. I had not shaken his hand once since being at the church.

Over time, my relationship with the pastor began to grow more and more. I would eventually work for him as his assistant. He traveled often, and I would join him on occasion. I would have the privilege of being around him, listening to how he governed, watching him lead, and seeing him vulnerable. That was a coveted position that often drew a great amount of envy from those inside and outside the group as well.

In reading Joseph's story, I could relate a little with it. The big glaring difference was that the pastor was not my father, and the other men were not my brothers. I felt like the oddball on most outings. I felt like they did not like me and desired any way they could to get rid of me. Some of that fear was in my mind, but it was still very real to me. Like Joseph, I did not strive to be alone with my brothers, and I would take much of the information I learned about them back to the pastor. I knew I had his ear, and I used it as much as I possibly could. This did not make my brothers like me. I was tolerated, at best.

As the story moves along, Joseph told his family about two dreams he had. The first dream was about eleven sheaves of wheat bowing down to his, and the second was about the sun, the moon, and eleven stars bowing to him as well. Both dreams could easily be interpreted to mean that Joseph would eventually rule over his family (Genesis 37:5-11).

Imagine that you have ten older brothers, and one of your brothers is treated as though he is the favorite. Think of all the animosity and bitterness that would grow in your heart. You work hard at being a great child, but you're not recognized for it. But, he is given the special treatment. He is always around your father while you are out herding the sheep with the rest of your brothers. You would get angry. Well, this happened to Joseph. His brothers became very jealous of him, and they conspired to ambush him.

They invited him on a shepherding trip to kill him. They wanted to get rid of him forever. But Joseph was spared this fate. They captured him and placed him in the pit until they figured out what to do with him. This is very significant because in that day having a son was very important. You might say that it was good for Jacob because he had many sons. Yes, he did, but there was only one son that was touched by God. None of the other sons could take his place.

To remove a son was a serious offense. Unlike Cain, the brothers did not kill Joseph. Their anger did not lead to bloodshed. However, they still wanted to be rid of Joseph, and they eventually realized that throwing him in the pit was not enough. Instead, they could gain a profit by selling him into slavery. This way he was out of their way for good. He is as good as dead. They sold him to the Midianites who in turn sold him to the Ishmaelites, who were heading to Egypt. They tore up the special coat Joseph received from his father, dipped it in goat's blood, and presented it to their father as proof of their brother's death. With Joseph out of the way, the brothers could seek to gain their father's attention.

This is something you will definitely encounter on your journey. Someone will be jealous and envious of you and your position. What you must realize is that God is the one who gives and takes away. He appoints and demotes. You did not get the position yourself. Many times, people desire a position they don't understand. To be a Joseph is a heavy responsibility. He is tasked with a big dream that carries a lot of significance.

I've heard sermons where preachers have said, "This is proof that you should not tell others your dreams." I do agree that we must be very responsible with the revelation and information we are given. I also agree that God's visions cannot be taken lightly, but I also believe that God will bring to pass whatever He chooses. God gave the dream; therefore, there was no one or nothing that could stop it from happening. His family would bow down to him one day.

You have to make sure that you don't become bitter and resentful at the people you have been called to serve. I don't mean to spoil the story for you, but Joseph's family does bow to him eventually. However, he does not pervert his leadership. Instead, he sees it as a privilege to serve. He could have had his brothers cast in the deepest, darkest prison, but he did not. God would use him to bless his brothers—the same men who sought to get rid of him. Hallelujah! You will have that same opportunity.

As a pastor, I am confronted with that dilemma daily. I am lied on, talked about, mistreated, misunderstood, and chastised. It can be tough, but I have resisted taking the bait of offense. I cannot do it. John Bevere has a great book about offense that I encourage all the pastors I cover in ministry to read. It is called *The Bait of Satan*. I implore you to get it. It exposes the dangers of offense and provides practical solutions. In fact, it has helped me a lot. I have sat in hospital rooms waiting for the same church member who gossiped about me to get out of emergency surgery so I could pray with him. I have sat in counseling sessions seeking to reconcile a marriage where both the husband and wife mistreated my family. The opportunity to retaliate will always be there, but you must resist it. Retaliation puts your leadership ability in jeopardy of being perverted and misunderstood. Your vision will become cloudy, and your mission will be tainted. Resist it, and get free from any hurt in your heart. And don't allow for the things that happened to continue to cause you to be upset.

Like the brothers did with Joseph, those who hate you will manipulate what you were favored with to use as evidence of your downfall and death. The brothers ripped up the garment and dipped it in blood. Your enemies will use what you were given as evidence of your downfall. "See, pastor, he's not even doing great with it! You should have given it to me. I can do better in that position!" They will use whatever they can to validate their insecurities and try to prove that God's hand is not on you. What they fail to realize is that it will not work! They can throw you in a pit, but God will make a way for you to get out. They will tear up your special garment, but God will restore you with garments fit for royalty. They will bring up accusations, but none of their words will last or stand. Be sure of it! I know from experience.

After Joseph was sold into slavery, he lived a very difficult life in Egypt. He was sold as a slave to Potiphar, a wealthy Egyptian merchant. Potiphar loved him greatly. I like to believe that it would have been difficult for Potiphar not to favor Joseph because God's hand was on him. This goes to show you that it does not matter where you go, the favor doesn't depart. Joseph began to attract the attention of Potiphar's wife, and she tried to seduce him. He was a handsome man, and the master's wife desired him. Genesis 39:12 reads, "And she caught him by his garment, saying, 'Lie with me!' And he left his garment in her hand and fled, and went outside." Yes, Joseph left quickly. Feeling embarrassed, she said to the men in her household, "See, he has brought in a Hebrew to us to make sport of us; he came in to me to lie with me, and I screamed." She made it seem like Joseph tried to rape her. That was not the truth. You can fully expect for people around you to tell lies on you.

Ultimately, he was thrown in prison. Don't make the mistake of thinking the prison was like an American prison. There was no cable television and meals throughout the day. It was a nightmare fit for the vilest criminals. Joseph did not deserve to be there. Maybe you have been in a situation where someone lied on you. I had a friend who was given a great position in a company he felt like he was supposed to work for. I was so proud of him. He was shown favor within the company, which eventually led to him rising in the ranks. He was promoted many times within the company, and the CEO favored him. Unfortunately, this attention brought on a lot of jealousy.

An employee that really did not like him—and she made it very clear she did not—started a lie that my friend was stealing from the company. She used a text message he sent to her that referenced a bad deal being made in the company to frame him. With no factual evidence to go on, the accusations and gossip soared up through the leadership. The CEO and Human Resources director called my friend into his office to let him know that he would have to let him go. My friend was hurt beyond measure. He felt like his destiny was tied to that place. He felt like God had forgotten about him and the favor had run out. He was distraught. He finally had to come to grips with what had happened. And he had to learn that lies, and false accusations will not detour God's plans.

He stayed without a job for many months. He faced several eviction notices, but his faith didn't falter. He continued to trust God. After months of praying and hoping, he was awarded a job that was far better than what he would have ever imagined. Through it all, he learned to trust God. This is a lesson you will have to learn as well. This is because God is with you.

Genesis 39:21 reads, "But the Lord was with Joseph and extended kindness to him, and gave him favor in the sight of the chief jailer." It's important to understand that as long as God is with you, it doesn't matter who leaves or joins you. While imprisoned, Joseph interpreted dreams, and he became very useful. He predicted that the butler would be exonerated in three days and restored to Pharaoh's service. He also interpreted the dream of the baker letting him know he would be put to death. Both interpretations came true.

Some time passed, and Pharaoh had a dream. The butler that escaped death and returned to the service of the royal house remembered his own situation. The Pharaoh desired a dream interpreter, and the butler told him about Joseph interpreting his dreams. So, Joseph was called to interpret it. He told the Pharaoh, "Seven years are coming, a great abundance through the land. Then seven years of famine will arise." This prompted Pharaoh to prepare Egypt for famine. Because of the hand of God being on him, Joseph was appointed second-in-command to Pharaoh. He was installed as the administrator over the nation where he was once imprisoned. Some might say he was promoted because of his ability to interpret dreams. I prefer to say that it didn't matter what his gifting was, it was by simply God's hand that he was promoted. God could have used his ability to mow grass to promote him. The focus should not be on the gift, but the Giver. You will fall and fail if you assume the gift is the promoter. It isn't. God lifts and destroys. He plants and uproots. The gift is for service; the Giver is for all things pertaining to life and godliness, which includes promotion and demotion.

I would think that Joseph was excited the moment he learned that he would be taken from the prison to the palace. Consider his life up to that point. He went from being in his father's presence to thrown in a pit to serving Potiphar to being cast in a prison until he was promoted to the palace.

Ultimately, the famine Joseph predicted happened, which brought his father and brothers to Egypt. They had to make the journey if they desired to live because they needed food. Joseph noticed his brothers, but he hid his identity to test his family (Genesis 42:33-34). More than twenty years had passed since they sold him into slavery. Although reluctant to release his last son, Benjamin, to the mysterious man's requests, Jacob relents. Upon seeing Benjamin Joseph revealed himself to his brothers, forgives them, and brings them all down to Egypt. Isn't it something that he recognized his brothers, but they didn't recognize him? Could it be that their wrongdoing and unrepentance held them back from progression? Notice that without Joseph they didn't fare any better. They removed him out of spite and envy. They meant for his life to be over and for him to be gone forever, but God had other plans. This can apply to your life as well. Your enemies can desire for your life to be over, but God will have the final say. They will cast you from their presence, but you won't just go away. No, you will develop and grow beyond their ability to recognize you. This is because they expect to see you as a slave, but they will see you as a ruler. They expect to see you slaving on the field, but they will find you in the palace.

It is awesome how God places you in a position that you won't even be able to understand. You didn't ask for it. He gave it to you. And you can trust that He has prepared the place He's shown you in the dream. Joseph saw his dream become a reality. His brothers bowed down to him (Genesis 43:26). What's interesting is in verse 32 Joseph, and his brothers sat at separate tables. I believe that verse is also prophetic in the sense that it shows the separation that must occur with you and those you're around—including your family. There will come a time when God will desire you to Himself. This does not mean you will necessarily have to physically leave everyone. Some may experience that, but I do not believe that is everyone's story. However, there will come a time when your thinking and methods are different. They will want to go in one direction, but God is leading you in another. You might be ridiculed or rejected, but you must know that it can be a normal part of the process.

My wife and I have hosted conferences all around the world. What we are most fascinated with are the people we have the pleasure of meeting. We started to notice a common trend amongst some of the people who attend our conferences. They were coming without their family's approval. Their family members were not Christians, so they created a story to attend our event. One young lady told us she asked her parents if she could visit a university in London, which happened to be the location for one of our events on our tour that year. She convinced her parents to allow her to fly from Paris to London alone to view a potential university she would attend. They allowed her to do it. To avoid lying, she went to the University, but her main reason for coming was to attend our conference. She wept as she talked about her family. It was truly heartbreaking. It was obvious that she and her family were sitting at separate tables. They were not on the same page spiritually, but that did not stop her from doing what she believed God was compelling her to do.

Genesis 45:3 reads "'I am Joseph!' he said to his brothers. 'Is my father still alive?' But his brothers were speechless! They were stunned to realize that Joseph was standing there in front of them." He then tells them not to be upset and angry with themselves for selling him into slavery. His reasoning for why is stunning. Some would assume that Joseph's brothers were responsible for the mess in his life. If that is true, then they would also be responsible for his promotion. This is because there is no palace without a pit.

No, the brothers were merely pawns in God's great game of chess. Joseph makes it clear who was responsible for what happened in his life. He says to his brothers, "It was God who sent me here ahead of you to preserve your lives." "God has sent me ahead of you to keep you and your families alive and to preserve many survivors. So, it was God who sent me here, not you! And he is the one who made me an adviser to Pharaoh—the manager of his entire palace and the governor of all Egypt." Wow! He said God was responsible. That is revelation. We can be so quick to believe that someone or something was responsible for the events in our life, but it is God. He is in full control, and He knows what He is doing. No one desires to be in the pit or the prison. Everyone desires the palace because it is comfortable and fulfilling. However, you must realize that the pit and the prison prepare you for the palace. Trust God through all of life's ups and downs. Like Joseph, God is ahead of you preparing the way and preserving the call He's given you. Do not be surprised when God sends you ahead to preserve the lives of others. The suffering you endure is nothing compared to the hope you're able to bring in a time of trouble.

The last thing I want to highlight about this story is Joseph's response to his brothers. He told them that it was God who sent him there to preserve their lives. Notice that he could have been filled with rage and anger at his brothers. Think how you would have reacted after seeing your brothers—the men who sold you into slavery—after 20 years. That is some heavy stuff. He had as much power as Pharaoh according to Genesis 44:18. He could have thrown them in jail or, even worse, had them killed. But he did not. Instead, he preserved their lives. He completed the will God had for him without envy and strife. I am sure his brothers were glad he was not filled with the same bitterness and hatred that filled their hearts. I am sure they were thankful he was not vengeful.

Pay attention when I tell you that you must be free from the people who have hurt you. You must be free from people so you can freely serve them. Aren't you glad Joseph didn't take his pain into his position like so many leaders tend to do? If he had, this story would have been different. I'm not even sure that God would have allowed him to leave the pit or the prison until his heart was clean and forgiving. Is yours? As Joseph went higher, some would expect that he would become more hurtful. But he did the opposite. Will you?

My friend, the palace may be your destination, but the pit is purposeful. If God is preparing you for a position, trust that He knows the journey you should take. It will not look like you think it should. And that's okay. Trust Him.

SHIFTING SEASONS

Seasons come and go. You will go through seasons of sowing, reaping, tests and trials, mourning, joy, and so many more. However, I believe there are four seasons of the Lord. There is a season of fighting, one of resting, another of sowing, and one of reaping. You will encounter all of these seasons many times throughout your journey. There will be times when it is very dry. It will seem like nothing is working, the connections are gone, and all seems lost. I know about this season because I have lived through it many times. I became depressed because of it. I lost hope in the midst of it. I felt like I had done something to cause God to dry up my free-flowing rivers. Did I say something? Did I not do something He asked of me? I would quickly dismiss grace and go directly to legalism. I made God out to be someone who awarded His blessings based on good behavior as if I would be worthy of anything He did for me. Don't make this mistake.

When God lays His hand on you, He does it because it is His desire, not yours. He touched you in your mother's womb and put words in your mouth before you mumbled your first word. He chose you, not the other way around. Don't think for a second that your deeds moved Him. He foreknew you, and it was then that He chose you. The dry season is not an indication of His lack of love for you. Rather, it is a sign of the times. And you must learn how to tell the times in order to be successful in every season of life.

Genesis 8:22 reads, "As long as the earth remains, there will be planting and harvest, cold and heat, summer and winter, day and night." I want you to pay very close attention to planting and harvesting. Some translations refer to planting as seedtime. Either way, the time to plant and the time to harvest are significant times you must know and recognize. The first thing you must notice is that it will not go away as long as the earth remains. You can expect this season in your life as long as you live. Sowing isn't always fun.

I grew up with a garden behind my house. It was painstakingly horrible to maintain. I had to cultivate the ground, plant the seeds, water them on occasion, monitor their growth, pick the weeds around it, and so much more. The task was demanding. It required a lot of effort, and it was frustrating. I wanted to see fruit, but day after day I saw nothing. Then, I would see a little leaf emerge through the soil and had a little hope that something was growing. Days later, it would get a little bigger until the fruit started to bud. Time would pass, and I'd see more and more fruit. The most painful part was waiting to see what I was hoping for. The period before the harvest was dry—very dry.

I've encountered times in ministry where everything seemed to just shut down. People would stop coming to the church. Those who came stopped giving. I was no longer receiving invitations to preach. My books were not selling. My businesses were not operating efficiently. My bills were increasing, but my funds were decreasing. It was a very tough time, and I did not know another way out. I wanted to cry most days because I had to fight the feeling that maybe God had forgotten about me. Maybe He was no longer concerned about my wellbeing or desires. I felt like I was sitting in a desert searching for answers and provision. "God, where are you?" That was my question most days. "I am serving you faithfully, but I see nothing. All I'm doing is sowing, but I see nothing happening." It was after that statement that my life changed. I realized what was going on. I was in a season of preparation. What was I preparing for? I was preparing for the harvest, and it is the season when you are able to collect all you've been sowing.

The seasons will change before your eyes, but you won't always realize it. First Chronicles 12:32 reads, "From the tribe of Issachar, there were 200 leaders of the tribe with their relatives. All these men understood the signs of the times and knew the best course for Israel to take." This is a profound idea and essential to your journey. To "know" in this verse is the word "yada," which means "God gives personal understanding and revelation." This personal revelation is different from what you can learn by reading a book. When the Bible talks about revelation, it is the revealing of something or someone. Things that were hidden are revealed. It is as if something or someone is being unveiled because you would not have known it otherwise.

Think about someone telling you they got you a new car. You show up, but all you see is a red curtain. You can believe by faith that the car is there, but it has yet to be unveiled. Jesus is our revelation because He tore the veil that once separated us from the Father. Hallelujah! Jesus reveals Himself as God, and He leaves us with the Holy Spirit. Peter had a lesson in revelation in Matthew 16:13-20. Jesus asked His disciples who men said He was. That's an important question you will have to ask those around you one day if you have not already. Knowing who you are is valuable, and knowing who others think you are can be just as valuable. However, being controlled by what people think about you is not healthy. Asking those around you who you are allows you to identify your outward influence. You are allowing those around you to assist you in identifying your total influence, which is a mixture of who you are to yourself and who others think you are.

The next question Jesus asked was who He was to them. Peter responded in verse 16, "Thou art the Christ, the Son of the living God." Jesus makes it clear that no man could have revealed that to Him. God revealed Himself to Peter, and that revelation changed His life. This goes to prove that God can and will reveal what is necessary for you to know. He will not leave you in the dark.

By virtue of revelation, those who are capable of discerning the seasons can distinguish between what is wise and unwise. This anointing, or supernatural ability, is gained through intimacy with God. It is in the intimacy of prayer that they can receive wisdom, so they're able to seize on opportunities. It should be noted that God has provided many opportunities, but only a few have been able to discern them. The doors have been opened, but some have been too busy worrying about everyone else's business that they didn't walk through them. Many are so focused on what everyone else is saying that they couldn't discern God's guidance.

By discerning the season, you will know if it is the right time to make the right move. These special men and women can foresee revival, financial collapse, miracles, and God-opportunities that escape others. They can discern what God is doing so they are able to encourage others to walk with Him.

Understanding the seasons allows for you to know when it is the time to reap and the time to sow. The problem is that too many people attempt to reap when they should be sowing. They are trying to eat the blades of grass because they are too impatient to wait for the fruit to mature. They eat the seeds instead of waiting for the harvest. This is not a good practice because once the seeds are consumed, there is no hope. Fruit will produce seeds, but caution to the man or woman who has eaten his or her seed. They will be left with nothing to grow.

I arrived at a Bible study one evening prepared to teach an important sermon. I taught on what I believed to be an oncoming financial collapse. I encouraged them to get out of debt, store up as much cash as possible, and place full trust in the Lord. I elected to take questions that evening. One gentleman asked me, "Pastor, that doesn't sound right. Everything seems to be going well right now. The housing market is the best it has ever been. I'm selling houses right and left. The stock market is the highest it has been in years. I just don't understand why you're saying that we should be saving instead of spending. It doesn't sound right." I understood what he was saying, but I prayed that God would illuminate his understanding. See, you don't spend wildly when everything is going well. That's the time to save. You save while you have the job, so you aren't financially dependent if you lose it. I challenged him with this question: "If the market is high, where does it have the potential to go next?" He said, "Down, possibly." I accepted that answer, and I conversed with him about having spiritual eyes to see and to discern the times. I saw it because God revealed it to me, and that night I learned that some might not see it.

I've had to live with that reality. It became so apparent years ago when I drove through downtown Atlanta during one of the worst financial recessions of our day. I noticed cranes and construction workers. It hit me like a ton of bricks. Why were companies building new things if we were in the middle of a recession? It didn't make sense. Then, God revealed it to me. Everyone doesn't recess in a recession. They properly understood the times and spent wisely. They were good stewards of their money, and they were able to capitalize on the low costs during the recession. They were buying buildings and land that was once too expensive to walk on. They saw it, but millions of people didn't. That was a shifting moment in my life. It was during that car ride that I asked God always to give me eyes to see. I didn't want to be left out in the dark. I had to discern the times.

Proper discernment enables you to open the right doors at the right time. Simply put, when it's God the plans will fall into place. If you are trying to do something in life that you believe God is telling you to do, then the proper provision will be there. He will provide the wood for the ark, as He did with Noah. He will provide the ram for the sacrifice, as He did with Abraham. He will provide the raven at the brook, as He did for Elijah. Ultimately, you will see the provision in the midst of chaos. However, if all you see are roadblocks, obstacles, constantly closed doors, massive resistance, and insurmountable pressure, then you should reevaluate your timing and evaluate the season you're in.

God could give you a vision that requires you to train before seeing it. He will show you a glimpse of it every so often to keep you encouraged. He will send laborers along your path to validate that you're going the right way. But if you see red flags, road blocks, and protective barriers, yield immediately! This could be God protecting you from something outside of His timing. What you're pursuing could be within God's will, but He will do whatever He can to make sure you're moving in His timing. He saves you from weariness, defeat, and distress. If it is God, then Grace will meet you there.

Have you ever had someone tell you not to quit? Well, I have. I've also told other people that. How would you feel to know that there are times in your life when you must quit? Being able to discern the seasons allows you to know what to quit and what to continue. The church my wife and I started in Mississippi had to be shut down. Imagine if we were unable to discern accurately. We would probably still be there trying to make something happen.

Think about the people you know who are still digging in the same hole God told them to leave years ago. The signs have been there. The provision is gone. The vision is absent. The mission is nonexistent. They are just digging a hole, and they refuse to quit because of either what others would say or because they don't want to be seen as quitters. Free yourself! If the signs are there for you to quit, quit! God will reveal it to you.

I tried running for political office several times, but I never quite got off the ground with the campaigns. It was heartbreaking because I wanted it to work. I desired to run for political office ever since seeing Bill Clinton being sworn into office back in 1992. I was intrigued by what I saw. I was 5 at the time. My last attempt at a political career was a potential run for a seat on the city council. I arrived at a potluck the councilmen were hosting so I could meet my potential opponents. To my surprise, the men knew me. One of the councilmen approached me and said, "Well, do you want the good news or the bad news first." I said, "Give me the bad news." "Well, the bad news is you live outside the city limits, which means you won't be able to run for this seat." I said, "What's the good news?" He said, "The good news is that you won't take my seat." I was heartbroken. I did not want to quit on my dream, but all of my options had run out. The signs were written on the wall. I continued to ignore them until I couldn't ignore them any longer. After the potluck, I went home and crawled into bed. I was frustrated. I had thrown my Bible against the wall and gotten very close to cursing God. I started to fall asleep until I heard the still voice of God say, "If you aren't going to do what I called you to do, why should I open your eyes in the morning?" My eyes opened wide, and I jumped out the bed. My heart was racing. I said, "God, forgive me! I'll do it. I'll preach Your word. I submit." I needed to quit my will for His.

Often, the evidence is there. Maybe the people have stopped calling you back and answering your emails. The provision has all but dried up. There is nothing left but you and the shovel you're digging with. God has given you the signs. Don't ignore them. It is very important to know how to discern the signs because they could indicate that you need to keep going. I know that can sound confusing, but that is only because we like to reduce God to formulas. We want to know exactly what He does and how He does it every time for everyone. It does not happen that way. He could be testing you to see if you will continue digging in the hole after everyone has left. You must discern your own signs and believe that He will reveal and illuminate your way.

We desire for God to fit into our formulas. We try to copy someone else's story without experiencing their seasons. It is dangerous to step out on someone else's word for your life! And it is equally dangerous to step out on someone else's word they received from God. Trying to duplicate someone else's exact story is one of the quickest ways to ruining your own. The biblical foundation and righteous standards of the stories should be similar, but to match exactly the points of someone else's story does not mean you will have their outcome. You should never be afraid to step out in the right season, and you should trust that grace will meet you there. Having faith that God can is more than sufficient for your journey. For those who try to convince you of what God can't do, ask them to show you what He hasn't done. All you need is a precedent, which is a legal decision that provides an example to guide you in any case! You must forecast properly concerning the seasons. You must know when to plant and when to sow.

Most people spend their time reaping in the season they are supposed to be sowing. You will always be prepared for a new season if you did what God asked of you in the prior season. For example, if you planted seed in the Spring and Summer, then you will be ready to reap a harvest in the Fall! Most people desire God to rain down provision. Here's the question everyone must consider: "If God gave you provision, where would you store it and how would you spend it?" He gives the shovel and ability to dig the stream and build the dam; God provides the rain/flood! But woe unto Him who fails to build before the coming rain. He'll drown in what He should have floated on. Many people believe God can give them a pond, but they turn away the opportunity because all they see is a shovel!

There are three themes in the Lord's seasons. The first is seed—time—harvest. Very few see the value of starting the foundation of something now without seeing the fruit of it until later. Sowing is difficult. It requires hard labor and consistency. You will sweat and sweat and sweat some more. Consider how you would feel if God told you to dig a hole. He gave you no other instructions except to dig. After months of digging, He told you to stop. You put the shovel aside, and He tells you to plant some seeds. "That's all, God? You had me dig just to plant a seed?" You're tired from digging and sowing, but the process isn't over. Now you have to wait. The harvest is coming, but first, there's time. You must wait until it comes. Can you be faithful to sow even if it means you may never reap?

The second theme is patience. Can you remain still long enough for training and instruction? Some people will desire to move in a hurry. They want to outrun God. Understand what I am saying. I am not implying that you can outrun God. You cannot. However, some like to think they can. Instead of remaining still for the next set of instructions, they run.

The third theme is knowing how to exit a season respectfully. I have experience in doing it the wrong way. The way you leave your current situation will trickle into the conditions of the next. As I mentioned in an earlier chapter, I worked for a church for almost four years. Towards the end of my tenure there I grew angry and bitter. I resented the staff and the pastor. I felt wronged and used. Instead of dealing with my emotions, I reacted based on how I felt. I was harsh and unloving. I resigned, and I didn't look back. I gave just enough back to get away. I refused to assist any more than what was required. I left that season the wrong way. I gossiped, lied, and brought confusion. Can you tell what happened to me five years later? THE SAME THING! The only difference was I was on the other side of the table. I was the pastor being lied on and talked about. I vowed then that I would never sow those seeds again. I received my harvest. It was not what I wanted, but it was definitely what I got. I learned a valuable lesson in how to exit one season and enter a new one. You enter and exit with thanksgiving, humility, and love. Leave the criticism, pride, and selfishness out. Don't plant it, or you will see a harvest of it.

There are four primary seasons of the Lord. The first is the season of fighting and hard work. This is where you must grab your sword of the Spirit, which is the Word of God, and your shield of faith to go to battle. You must grab your hammer and nails to go to work. It's a tough season because it requires a great amount of energy. You are often tired, but you cannot quit fighting and working. You will be expected to build with one hand and fight with the other. You will lay the foundation one day while keeping your enemies from destroying it the next. Many quit during this season because hard work and dedication is required. And many do not like hard work.

The second season is resting. That is where you are finished fighting and working. God requires you to wait on Him. You will live out the words of Psalm 46:10, "Be still, and know that I am God! I will be honored by every nation. I will be honored throughout the world." You will also realize the words of 2 Chronicles 20:15-17, which reads,

> He said, 'Listen, all you people of Judah and Jerusalem! Listen, King Jehoshaphat! This is what the Lord says: Do not be afraid! Don't be discouraged by this mighty army, for the battle is not yours, but God's. Tomorrow, march out against them. You will find them coming up through the ascent of Ziz at the end of the valley that opens into the wilderness of Jeruel. But you will not even need to fight. Take your positions; then stand still and watch the Lord's victory. He is with you, O people of Judah and Jerusalem. Do not be afraid or discouraged. Go out against them tomorrow, for the Lord is with you!

The king and the people bowed and praised the Lord. He delivered them from the hands of their enemies. They did not have to fight. Isn't that amazing? All they needed to do was rest! You will need to understand that season because it is very important. I failed that test the first time I took it. After I had dropped out of college, I continued going back and forth in prayer asking God to give me instructions. For an entire year, all I heard was: "Rest!" I was angry and felt like I was wasting away. Why would God want me to rest? I didn't understand it. After a year of failing to rest I finally started walking more in my purpose. I started my job at the church, and I was exhausted daily. After two months on the job I prayed and asked God to help me. His response, "I told you to rest." I just got up from my knees and went to bed. I was disobedient, and I was eating the fruit of it in the new season.

The third season is sowing. We have gone over that in some detail above, so I will not restate it again. The main point I want to highlight about this season is servanthood. You must learn the importance of being a servant. The most valuable thing you sow is your time. You will give without seeing anything in return. You will give without knowing if anything will be given back. It will seem like you are being abused and taken advantage of. You will have just enough to get by, but you must continue sowing. Never forget that the measure you give is the measure you receive. This means sowing with a large measure means you will reap in large measure.

The fourth and final season is reaping. This is where you see the harvest. The temptation in this season is to eat what you collect instead of saving it for the famine. The purpose of the harvest is to store it for yourself and others! Remember that God placed His hand on you for His glory and the benefit of others. You are tasked with giving more because your net to receive is larger. You receive more to give more.

I had a young man tell me that he dreamed of building his own home one day. I encouraged him in his dream; then I challenged him. I said, "Why just your own house? Why not endeavor to build a community?" See building the house is great, but building a community means you're able to house other people. Your life becomes bigger than you. This is why God gives you a harvest!

I think of my own life. I am a little different than many of the preachers I know. Some prefer to remain completely separated from others. I don't. For years I preached a powerful sermon on Sunday morning, left the church, purchased groceries, and went home to cook a feast for anyone who wanted to come. I cooked chicken dressing, sweet potatoes, collard greens, mac and cheese, roast, baked chicken, blackened salmon, and everything you can think of. I did this every Sunday after church. There were some Sundays that I was too tired to eat. I did that because God instructed me to. He gave me the strength to do it. I saw it as feeding the people spiritually and physically. Ultimately, God was teaching me something about serving and rewarding others with the harvest He gave to me.

For years my wife and I have not lived in our home alone. Our children have been with us, but we have housed many people over the years. We allowed couples who were in domestic violence situations stay in our home. We welcomed some of our church leaders and friends. Through all it, we did not ask to be compensated. Our thought process was this: if God gave us an empty room, then He had someone to occupy it. One thing God knows about us is that we will fill an empty room. We operate and live within a village—our village. It is comprised of men and women we trust. Some are family by blood and others are family through the blood of Jesus. Our village is aware of one thing: when we eat, they eat! If I'm going to the store to purchase food, then it is going to be enough for the village. I understand that God placed His hand on me so I could help others. This applies to you too. Bless the people; feed His sheep.

Lastly, there are five ways to tell a new season has come.

The first is God revealing it plainly. John 8:12 reads, "He that follows Me shall not walk in darkness, but he shall have the light of life." The Holy Spirit reveals the things of God to us.

The second is through significant life events that bring major life changes to your normal routine. This could be a birth, graduation, death, destruction of something, the building of something, marriage, divorce, or the like. These things are indications that a shift is taking place. You are about to enter a new season.

The third is when you begin to see old things and people leave your life. This can be a tough one. If you are going into pastoral ministry, prepare for this to happen often. Let me help you with something. If you look at your church like a prison, then you'll have inmates desiring to escape your wrath. That is not Christ's Bride. I like to tell our church that it is like a pasture with a revolving door. I don't mind if people leave my specific pasture. I just want to make sure they don't hop over the fence. When there's a mass of people leaving your life, prepare yourself for new people to come. You will have to build new bridges and tear down old walls. Don't run from this time; embrace it.

The fourth is recognizing that the grace has been lifted. You begin to make mistakes you usually don't make. Assignments that were once simple become very challenging and cumbersome. You lack motivation. You become restless, and it's as if you have no vision. You feel like a race horse being housed in a pasture. You want to run, but the fence keeps you bound. You feel out of place, and it becomes unbearable to stay in the season because it feels like you have outgrown it. When you sense these things, it is time for you to leave the nest. This is a sign from Heaven. It's time to make the shift into a new season.

The fifth and final indication is when the enemy begins to throw false signs to slow you down. He tries to make you afraid. He wants you to rely on yourself. When he becomes fearful of your next season, that means it's coming quickly. Brace yourself and prepare for what's to come.

All in all, you must be able to discern your seasons and trust God as you walk accordingly.

NO COMPARISON

I'd be remiss not to write a chapter on the dangers of comparison. We just learned about Joseph and everything he endured from the time he had a dream until it came true. I've read that passage many times, and I like to put myself in Joseph's shoes. I probably would have been very upset at God and harbored resentment towards my father and brothers. Why would I be upset with my father? Because I would have felt like he should have come to look for me. It may sound unreasonable, but that is how the enemy plays with your mind.

Why would I be upset with God? Well, for starters He gave me a dream that would take years to become a reality. That is frustrating! To go from such an encouraging dream to being thrown into a pit, sold into slavery by my brothers, lied on, and cast in prison just to reach the palace would have been absolutely horrible. Notice that Joseph had a glimmer of hope every now and then. He found favor with Potiphar, but it did not last long. It appeared as though God abandoned him. I could only imagine how I would have reacted in that moment. To be cast in jail after I was lied on would have been crushing. How would I be able to hold on to the dream after I have lived a nightmare?

I started my journey of faith asking God to give me a dream. He did. Then, I asked Him to show the way. I wanted Him to illuminate the process so I would not be surprised when things happened. I confessed James 1:5-6 by asking God for wisdom. I did not doubt He would give it, so I expected it. "God, show me the way!" That does not sound like a question, does it? This is because I did not really ask Him a question. I mostly demanded an answer, but I did not understand what I was asking for. I had to learn that God answers and rewards according to His perfect will. It was not in God's will for me to know everything. If I knew the entire story, I would not need Him! Why would I need to trust Him if I knew everything that was prepared to happen?

You should settle that issue in your heart as well. You cannot expect God to give you all the answers or to illuminate the entire way. Look at Abraham. He sent him to a place that he had no knowledge of. He gave David a vision, but it was not fulfilled for many, many years. God has a pattern in how He does things. He usually gives His servants a little information at a time. It is like solving a jigsaw puzzle. He gives one piece at a time until you have the pieces for a masterpiece. It can be frustrating because you want all the pieces at once. "Just give me all the pieces, God! Stop playing with my emotions!" That's what we want to say, but maturity and wisdom prompt you to step back and just have childlike faith. We must believe that our Holy God is fully aware of what will happen before it happens. We must trust Him throughout the entire process.

Nonetheless, comparison is one of the most dangerous things you can have on your journey. It robs you of having pure joy for others. It makes everything about you, and only you! You become the center of attention, and everything else is either better or worse than your situation. It takes your eyes off the main focus—which is to glorify God and be obedient to Him in all things—because you are so busy focused on everything and everyone else. You can also miss out on many things because you are not looking accurately and focusing on the important things. The reason I mentioned Joseph's story is because it is one that could have gone a different way if he had allowed comparison to pollute his heart. I'll place myself in his position to drive the point home.

If I were him, I would have possibly compared my situation with my brothers. While I was enslaved in a foreign land, my brothers were with our father living in freedom. While I was falsely accused of raping another man's wife, my brothers were eating what they desired. While I sat in jail, my brothers were enjoying their life without me. They won, and I lost! The enemy would have successfully polluted my heart with jealousy and envy until it transformed into anger and resentment. I would not have been of any good use until my heart was purged of all of its contaminants. I would have looked at my situation as if God was toying with me, dangling a carrot out in front me. It was close enough to see but too far to touch. That is an excruciating thought! Have you ever felt like that? Have you felt like God was toying with you? You probably feel that way right now—like He doesn't care anything about you. He showed you a vision only to snatch away any hopes of it ever being a reality.

There are two things I want you to do. You ready? First, I want you to ask yourself this question: "Can I still trust God even when I see the vision unraveling?" You might want to take a little time to think about the question and your answer. For some, they can respond with confidence that they will trust God no matter what. Others are not so sure. I can tell you that this journey is best lived knowing that you can trust God no matter how it looks or feels. I can tell you from experience that you will have moments where you feel like you are trapped in a pit, thrown in slavery, falsely accused, cast in jail, and unrecognizable. God does not tell us that things will not happen. He does not promise that we will never get in the furnace. What He promises is that He will always be there with us. No matter how hot the flames get, He will be there with us.

There was a time in my ministry when I felt trapped and alone. It felt like God abandoned me. It was as if He left me to wallow in my insecurities. Could He rescue me? Of course! Why He chose to leave me, so I thought, was beyond my understanding. I failed to realize that God had other plans. He was training me to prepare me for where I was going. Nevertheless, I started to compare my life and story with others. I saw many other men excelling, or so I thought. I felt like they were moving on in their life and accomplishing things while I was laying on my face in the closet. They were accepting speaking engagements while I was fasting and reading my Bible. They were preaching to crowds while I was sitting in an empty room. They were praising with others, and I was crying alone. I felt like God did not care anything about me. He gave me a vision, but it felt like no one around me could see it.

I will never forget the dream I had. I want to share it with you. In this dream, I was walking in a dry, desolate desert. The sun was beaming down on me, and I could barely walk due to exhaustion. I was thirsty and hungry, but I saw no relief for miles. As I climbed what looked like a steep hill, I saw the top of a palm tree. I hurried over the other side of the hill to find an oasis. The pond was filled with rich water, and it was surrounded by the best vegetation on this side of eternity. I rushed down to the still waters and started to drink until I was filled. I reached over and began eating the rich vegetation until I was full.

I knelt for a moment until I noticed a shadow on the other side of the pond. I looked over, and there was another person. I ran over, grabbed his hand, and led him to the brook to drink. I gave him food to eat. Then, I noticed others coming up the hill. I ran to help them get to the brook. I did this until it became too much for me to handle alone. I gathered many of people who had been at the brook for a while and asked them to help me. They were already filled, so I taught them the importance of helping the others find nourishment and provision. They would become the core team to assist the other people who were coming down to the brook.

There were some that I sent out into the desert. Why send them out? Because I knew there were other lost people wandering around looking for nourishment. It was a risky move, but I knew it would pay off in the long run. Some would not return, but others would come back with more people. As they drunk from the brook and ate, I'd implore them not to go back to their old way of living and be free at the oasis. We gathered, grew, and then it was time for them to go. They were commissioned to go back into the world to tell others what they found. It did not take me long to know what God was saying. The Oasis would soon become the name of our church—The Gathering Oasis Church. I saw people from all nationalities coming to the oasis. It was amazing.

The desert represented the world. It was dark, dry,

and desolate. It was lifeless, and it broke my heart that people were dying without hope while an oasis was close by. John 4:14 reads, "But those who drink the water I give will never be thirsty again. It becomes a fresh, bubbling spring within them, giving them eternal life." That was the oasis. It was rich in everything needed to sustain life.

I was baffled how God would set up a place of such beauty in a dark desert, but I did not have much time to think about it because the people were coming in droves. There were more people there than I could handle. There were many other layers to that dream, but I am sure you understand the point of it all.

I told my pastor the dream, and he listened. Unfortunately, he did not share my enthusiasm. I told others, but they did not believe it either. All I knew was that I had to find that oasis for myself. I thought I needed to go build it, but God said to me, "I'll show you the place." That was the beginning of my pastoral journey.

The church would not be formed until almost two years later. Yes, years passed before we had our first service. We started the church in Jackson, Mississippi. After spending thousands of dollars on advertising and marketing for our first service, no one showed up except my family and another couple. I was heartbroken. I felt like God showed me that great dream only to abandon me. I did everything I knew to do. I was losing hope. In the back of my mind, I did not want to quit because I was concerned about what others would say. I saw other pastors starting their churches with crowds of people. Maybe I missed God! Maybe the dream was not for me. I was not sure what to do next. I just wanted to curl myself up into a big ball and die. Why would God toy with me like that? I couldn't understand it.

My wife and I closed down the church in Mississippi after God told us to move back to Atlanta, Georgia. In January of 2013, God refreshed my desire to start another church in our new hometown. We started The Gathering Oasis Church in Atlanta, Georgia. After everything that happened before I was weary about what would happen this time. However, I pressed on, trusting that this was God's plan for my life. As at the time of writing this book, we are still going strong. But, it has not been easy.

We have had many ups and downs. We started the church in a movie theater. It had mice that ran around the floor during service. After it rained, it would smell like mold and mildew. The environment was very liberal. No one would think that it was a suitable place for a church. Thankfully, God remained with us. We went from the theater to a church, which was over an hour away from where we lived at the time. It was a nice property, but it was further out than where we were before. We lost many of our gatherers due to the move. Numbers dropped, and bills were increasing. We were paying a very high amount for the building, but we felt like God led us there. We were told to vacate the building, and we only had 60 days to find a new location. We rented a hotel ballroom, Galleria ballroom, and a school amphitheater. We used classrooms, the cafeteria, and the gym. We learned how to be flexible and trust God. Through all of these moves, it looked like the vision would not come to pass. However, as you read this book, I can tell you that I have seen many small glimpses into the dream, but I have not realized it in totality.

God has given me many other dreams. I've had glimpses of that reality. They were short bursts of what is to come. I love those moments because they encourage me to keep going. Consider the tale of two mice. A scientist placed two mice in vases in separate, dark rooms. He filled both vases halfway with water. The only difference was that he turned on a small light in one of the rooms that shined directly on one of the mice. It was not a big light, but a small beam. The mouse in the completely darkened room died within hours. The mouse in the room with a small beam of light lived for more than two days.

The scientist questioned the reason why the mouse with a small beam of light lived longer. The answer was clear. He had hope! The small beam of light gave him a bit of hope to stay alive. The moments God gives you in your life are purposed to give you hope. The short glimpses into your future are used to encourage you to continue forward. Don't despise those moments. God is using them, and they're for your good.

Please understand that the vision God has given you is for His glory. There is absolutely no comparison between you and anyone else. Don't try to mimic someone else's story. Don't try to duplicate someone else's gifts. God made you an original, so do not die a copy.

You can follow others as they follow Christ, but do not try to be them. The only One we seek to imitate fully is Jesus. There is no comparison with you. Stop trying to compare your life with others. Your journey will not look the same. Your process will not be similar. The foundational principles will be similar, but don't confuse that with the rest I have said above.

You will have the same faith, pray the same prayers, and hope in the same God, but the journey you travel will have different destinations. When you compare you belittle, and you have very little time to belittle what God is doing in your life. Trust Him. He is faithful to finish what He has started in you, around you, and through you.

LEAVING EGYPT

Exodus 16:2-10 details the events about how God's chosen people, the Israelites, escaped Egypt and Pharaoh's bondage. Although free, the people begin to complain to Moses, their leader, about their conditions in the wilderness. They would rather go back to their bondage in Egypt than remain free people in the wilderness. Let's look at how it happened.

There, too, the whole community of Israel complained about Moses and Aaron. "If only the Lord had killed us back in Egypt," they moaned. "There we sat around pots filled with meat and ate all the bread we wanted. But now you have brought us into this wilderness to starve us all to death." Then the Lord said to Moses, "Look, I'm going to rain down food from heaven for you. Each day the people can go out and pick up as much food as they need for that day. I will test them in this to see whether or not they will follow my instructions. On the sixth day they will gather food, and when they prepare it, there will be twice as much as usual." So, Moses and Aaron said to all the people of Israel, "By evening you will realize it was the Lord who brought you out of the land of Egypt. In the morning, you will see the glory of the Lord, because he has heard your complaints, which are against him, not against us. What have we done that you should complain about us?" Then Moses added, "The Lord will give you meat to eat in the evening and bread to satisfy you in the morning, for he has heard all your complaints against him. What have we done? Yes, your complaints are against the Lord, not against us." Then Moses said to Aaron, "Announce this to the entire community of Israel: 'Present yourselves before the Lord, for he has heard your complaining.'" And as Aaron spoke to the whole community of Israel, they looked out toward the wilderness. There they could see the awesome glory of the Lord in the cloud.

The Israelites were proving themselves to be extremely unthankful. Moses was very quick to remind them that their complaints were ultimately against God, not him and Aaron. Ungratefulness is one of the many impediments to progress in the purposes of God. It tells God that you do not appreciate your current state of being, as if what you have now and where you are now didn't come from Him! Whether you feel like you are in a wilderness—a very dry place—or in the Promised Land—a place of provision—you should be thankful.

The apostle Paul thanks the church in Philippi for their generosity. He writes in Philippians 4:11-12, *"Not that I was ever in need, for I have learned how to be content with whatever I have. I know how to live on almost nothing or with everything. I have learned the secret of living in every situation, whether it is with a full stomach or empty, with plenty or little."* It is important not to miss what Paul is saying. He is not saying that he does not lack. He's only saying that he doesn't need anything more than what God provides. This is because he's content with whatever he has. Praise the Lord! That is true wealth and prosperity. The drama and dysfunction in Egypt desires to hold you back and keep you in bondage.

Dysfunction and drama—if one has lived in it for many years—can feel more desirable than freedom. Especially, when it is all you are used to. You must realize that what you had in abundance in your past still isn't beneficial. It was available, but it isn't profitable. For some, the difficulty of leaving the bondage and dysfunction behind can be overwhelming. For others, they find it a struggle not to go back to it. They would rather die in slavery than suffer a little in the wilderness, so they are able to experience the goodness of the Lord in the Promised Land. For them, freedom doesn't always look as exciting as bondage. They are walking through smoke and looking in mirrors to find what doesn't exist. Their bondage cries out to them. They have left their cell and walked outside the jail. Although free, their heart longs for what they left behind. I need you to realize that the temptation to go back is not worth it!

When you highlight what you're missing rather than realizing what you have, you minimize the One who took you out of the pit so you could experience the Promised Land. And when you complain about what you're going through and what you don't have in the wilderness, you fail to consider what God has provided for you. I know God's Hand is on you, and I know you desire to move forward. I just want you to stop complaining about where you are. Realize that your current experience doesn't define your future. Stop complaining and endure. Learn the process and pass the tests that ultimately prepare you for where you're going.

Egypt is a place of captivity, oppression, suffering, and slavery. It represents everything God opposes and shows a need of deliverance. The wilderness is a place of testing and temptation. It signifies what is little inhabited and cultivated. It's a place of relatively little life and light. The Promised Land is not necessarily an earthly place, but an eternal existence, peace, rest, and prosperity—a promised possession inherited completely by faith. It is a symbol of deliverance. I don't know where you currently find yourself, whether it's Egypt, the wilderness, or the Promised Land, just learn to be content.

Many find themselves in the wilderness, and they are missing Egypt. They've become addicted to dysfunction and chaos. They have been in it so long that it is all they are used to. Egypt is so dysfunctional that peace and sobriety scares them. It forces them to confront their reality, deal with their issues, and excel over their anxiety. And it can be hard to confront your reality. Peace and sobriety confront the dysfunction and challenges you to deal with your situations instead of ignoring them. The issues can be like an iceberg. Although the ice peak is small and almost unnoticeable, the structure underneath the water is enough to sink the largest ship. Many great men and women have sunk because they failed to confront the structure underneath. The sheet of ice on top of the water, the part that was visible, was deceiving. I implore you to realize the danger in not confronting the issues that have the potential of sinking you.

Learn how to confront the elephant in the room. You may enjoy, celebrate, and delight in dysfunction, drama, and bondage but doing this will never move you to where God is trying to get you. You could have been born and raised in dysfunction and other intergenerational forces, but you have to find a way to control the chaos, so it is manageable and learn how to function within it. Otherwise, they will continue to create confusion during overwhelmingly normal situations making it harder to manage your life. You will leave a good situation for something/someone more chaotic just to appease your deep seeded desire for chaos and dysfunction. Look at your life. Are you sitting in dysfunction? Are all your friends feeding your need for drama and chaos? Have you gotten to a place in life where you do not desire change? You like the idea of it, but not the implementation of it. So, this begs the question: "Why are you reading this book?"

Does it pain you to hear about the Promised Land, which is a place of deliverance, but never walk towards it, accept it, or call out to it? Is it not enough that the dysfunction you were raised in is prevalent in your life and trickling down to your children? Have you sat to think what will happen if nothing changes? You fail to see the Promised Land because you are too busy focusing on and complaining about the wilderness and missing the bondage in Egypt. You hunger for the drama and dysfunction as if you are trying to get your next fix. It becomes the drug of choice, and like any addiction, you slowly build a tolerance for it that requires more of it to get the same effect. You'll need more and more around you, and if it does not happen naturally, then you must create it.

Egypt is on your television, playing through your radio and taking up space on your phone. You will attempt to fast away from it—a week without whatever show, song, or movie—until it begins to call out to you. Like a habit that must be fed, it screams out to you and beckons you until you give in to it. When dysfunction is your substance of choice, it can become difficult to keep friends. You will push everyone away until you're alone. Then, you will wonder why the people around you have left you. You will desire to be around people, but you look around and realize that you're all alone.

I know what bondage looks like because I've lived in it for years. I showered in it. I ate it. I watched it. I celebrated it. I watched programs on television that I should not have and listened to music that I should have abandoned. Dysfunction ran my life. If I had continued in it, I would not be where I am now. I would not be able to fulfill what God has called me to do and be who He has called me to be.

The presence of drama and dysfunction is powerful. It's changing your thoughts and affecting your life. You must back away from certain things. You must evaluate your music and what you're watching. You must stop listening to the music that promotes sex and perversion. You must remove yourself from any associations that push you to remain in bondage. Get away from it.

God's Hand is on you for a specific purpose and reason. I encourage you to escape the bondage of Egypt and be content where you are.

SUBMISSION TO AUTHORITY

This is probably one of the most important chapters you'll read in this book. Submission will be your greatest but most important test throughout your journey. I have many personal accounts of both success and failure when it comes to submission to authority. I am convinced that my journey stalled because I refused to submit to authority—the spiritual authority of my pastor.

In many cases, I was rude and acted immaturely. I said things I should not have and did things I should not have done. This test proved that I was not ready for a leadership position. I thought I was, as you probably assume for yourself right now. But before you seek the stage and lights, ask yourself if you are willing to submit where you are. If you cannot say you are, then put this book down and ask God to deal with your heart. You need to live out submission, and you start that with a desire to submit.

Submission can be broken down in two words, sub and mission. Sub is a prefix that means under, below, or beneath. It can also imply secondary and subordinate. Mission is defined as the business with which a group is charged or an important duty or task that is assigned. It means to be sent out for some duty or purpose. If we put these two words together, we see something remarkable. We're able to determine that submission is when one is able to get under or beneath an important duty or task assigned. It means you are able to get below and complete some duty or purpose. This definition implies that submission is comprised of two main elements—desire and action. You must first desire to be under the mission, and you must be willing to act out the important duty or assignment you've been assigned.

My wife and I host a marriage retreat yearly, and this subject is one of our most popular sessions. This is because many marriages struggle in the area of submission. The wife does not want to submit, and the husband refuses to love. Because there is no order, the marriage begins to break down, and a lot of confusion arises. The mission isn't clear anymore. The direction has been lost because neither spouse is clear on where he or she is going. The wife doesn't want to go left with her husband, and the husband refuses to go right. Therefore, they spend many years being angry and stuck in the middle. It is very discouraging to see. One significant thing about **submission is that it is for your protection**. It is also an **act of great strength**, not weakness. It is **for your training**.

Before I break down many of the important pillars of submission, I must deal with an important question concerning it. The question I am often asked is: "Would God desire for me to submit to unjust authority?" I believe 1 Peter 2:13-25 answers that question. It reads,

> *For the Lord's sake, submit to all human authority—whether the king as head of state, or the official he has appointed. For the king has sent them to punish those who do wrong and to honor those who do right. It is God's will that your*

honorable lives should silence those ignorant people who make foolish accusations against you. For you are free, yet you are God's slaves, so don't use your freedom as an excuse to do evil. Respect everyone, and love the family of believers. Fear God, and respect the king. You who are slaves must submit to your masters with all respect. Do what they tell you—not only if they are kind and reasonable, but even if they are cruel. For God is pleased when, conscious of his will, you patiently endure unjust treatment. Of course, you get no credit for being patient if you are beaten for doing wrong. But if you suffer for doing good and endure it patiently, God is pleased with you. For God called you to do good, even if it means suffering, just as Christ suffered for you. He is your example, and you must follow in his steps. He never sinned, nor even deceived anyone. He did not retaliate when he was insulted, nor threaten revenge when he suffered. He left his case in the hands of God, who always judges fairly. He personally carried our sins in his body on the cross so that we can be dead to sin and live for what is right. By his wounds you are healed. Once you were like sheep who wandered away. But now you have turned to your Shepherd, the Guardian of your souls.

That is a lot to digest. That is a passage that answers more of the question than you would hope it would. Nonetheless, we can clearly see that God fully expects us to submit even in unjust situations. As the scripture states, God called us to do good even when we are mistreated. He is pleased when we patiently endure unjust treatment. I know you might not want to read that, but it is important for you to know this for your journey. When unjust leadership arises—because it definitely will—you must be willing to submit anyway.

Jesus is our greatest example. He never sinned or deceived anyone, did not retaliate when he was insulted or seek revenge when He was threatened. He chose to allow God to fight His battle and bring about a fair verdict in heaven's courtroom. Submitting to unjust leadership is easier said than done. It takes everything in you to submit to someone who is mean and cruel towards you. However, God desires it from you. In fact, it pleases Him. Your act of submission is a show of love, grace, and mercy. You are extending to the leader what she or he does not deserve. She or he does not deserve your submission, but you are not doing it for him or her. You are doing it for the Lord.

I've served under many pastors throughout my short journey. I've had some good experiences and some that were not so great. No matter the pastor or situation, I was able to learn something from everything I experienced. Many of those experiences were not the best. I was very uncomfortable. I was told that I was stupid, put down for my youthfulness and inexperience, demeaned as a person, and so much more. I had to gauge their temperaments before approaching them. I wasn't sure exactly how I would be treated any given day. I had the worst anxiety before my day began. I would stop at a fast-food restaurant to vomit before driving onto the church campus because the stress level was just that high. I spent most of my days wanting to quit, but I knew I couldn't. This is because I live with the philosophy that quitting something God has told me to do is not an option. He sent me to serve the pastor for a reason, and I needed to fulfill and finish that part of my journey. I had to close that chapter of my life.

Please don't get me wrong; my service was not the best. I performed work with the wrong heart. I did not do it because I truly desired to serve. I did it out of survival sometimes. I did it to close the pastor's mouth or to make him pleased with me. I would perform the assignment, doing the least amount of work possible just to say I finished. Out of spite and bitterness, I purposely did not do many important tasks. While I smiled in the office, I complained and spoke evil towards him in private. My body was in a position to serve, but my heart was far away. I did not submit out of respect to God or patiently endured as I should have, and it's my hope that you avoid making the same mistake.

I freely admit that my time of service to my pastor at the time was one of the most difficult times in my life. I felt like I was receiving nothing out of it, but I can look back and tell that God had a greater plan. He destined something that I would not have ever been able to experience through my own logic. See, I would not have placed myself in a position where I felt emotionally abused and mistreated. I would not have willingly walked into a situation that did not seem comfortable. However, God has a way of doing things that you will not like but are for your benefit. I could not understand how the name-calling would help me, but it toughened my skin.

My wife and I lead several international ministries. We are a target for many enemies. We've been falsely accused and mistreated, but it doesn't bother us like it did in the beginning. We're both tougher mentally, emotionally, and spiritually than we have ever been, and most of that is due to our very rough and uncomfortable times serving very difficult leaders. My wife served as an intern for a large recording label. She was cursed out, put down, chastised for her faith, and so much more. But that treatment developed something in her that she could not learn in a classroom. No seminary class could have prepared either of us for the hell that would come against us and build in us with the endurance to continue despite it all. We learned so much from our experiences, but the most important lesson was learning how to submit when we did not want to.

My wife often recounts an experience between her and her boss. She was an intern at the time, and her boss was not a nice woman to her. It was a secular environment, so there was a lot of foul language and questionable activity. One day, as it got later and later into the night, my wife was still at work. You must remember that she was not being paid for what she was doing. God was teaching her a valuable lesson in service. While sitting at her desk, God told her to ask her boss if she wanted something to eat. My wife quickly told God she could not do it. It wasn't because she was physically incapable of doing it. No, it was because she didn't want to, which is how many of us are today.

She finally relented and asked her boss if she wanted something to eat. Remember it was very late at night, she was tired, and she did not want to do anything nice for someone who was so cruel towards her. Hoping her boss would decline the offer, she asked her again. Her boss told her that she did want something to eat, and she chose a restaurant that was on the other side of town.

That meant she had to get in her car and drive to get it. Now, that is uncomfortable!

It is important to point out that many times God will cause you do things that are uncomfortable to stretch you beyond your level of comfort. It is for your benefit. My wife drove to pick up the food only to come back to the office and have her boss tell her that she was not hungry. She was devastated, felt embarrassed, used, and mistreated. Nonetheless, she served and finished the job because it was her assignment. She is quick to tell others that she did what she did as unto the Lord, not her boss. She had to remember that her service had to be excellent because she was doing as if she was personally serving God. She had to override her emotions. They could not control her, and they cannot control you!

It is important to know that submission is for your protection. Consider marriage for a moment. First Peter 3:7 says that the woman is the weaker vessel. This does not mean she is inferior; rather she is valuable and worthy of honor. Value can be determined by the demand for the entity, or it can be given from its creator. Women are necessary for childbirth. If women ceased to exist, then reproduction as we know it would stop. God sees women of so much worth that He gave His life for their redemption—along with men. Women are worthy of respect. They deserve to be heard, understood, and given a position at the table. Men must understand that seeing women as partners does not lessen their own light. Rather, it allows the light to shine brighter. This is because men and women can do more together being mutually respectful than they can apart. She does not stand alone by herself. She is able to get under the mission of her husband as he submits under the mission of Jesus Christ. At no point is the husband and wife exposed to the extremities of the world without it first penetrating the armor of Christ. That is the foremost benefit of getting under someone or something.

Consider what happens when things are falling overhead. You quickly run to get under something that is strong enough to protect you. The covering is designed to provide ample protection so what is falling doesn't harm you. It protects the value and beauty of what it covers. This is the beauty of submission in marriage—the husband submitting to Christ as the head and the wife submitting to her husband as the head of their marriage.

You can also notice how God chose to protect women from their birth until death. Consider this. God shows how much He values women by protecting them from the womb to the grave. After a baby girl is born, she is placed under the authority and protection of her father. I have a little girl, and she pricks my heart. I want to protect her from everything. It is like I have her heart in my hands and I desire to make sure she is protected at all times. This is the responsibility of a father. I cover and protect her throughout her life until that moment comes along when she is engaged to her husband.

The marriage ceremony is very symbolic. I will walk her down the aisle and make a presentation to her husband. The minister will ask, "Who gives this bride away in marriage?" I will respond, "I do!" Well, I hope I'll respond that way. LOL. Nonetheless, I will hand my daughter's hand over to her husband, which is very symbolic. I am transferring her protection over to her husband. It is at that moment he is responsible for continuing the work I performed until that day. My daughter will be responsible for one thing, remaining submitted under my protection until she is married. Ultimately, it is for her protection. If something happens to a woman's husband and she's left as a widow, God does not leave her unprotected.

First Timothy 5:3 tells us to take care of the widows. Why? Because they are still valuable and vulnerable. The enemy will go after them first. They hold so much influence, and it must be protected. At no time does God leave a woman vulnerable and open for attack. She is tasked with submitting and being protected from the womb to the grave.

I did not see the beauty of submission and how it could be for my protection until later in my journey. Many of the things I felt my leaders told me to do were unreasonable, but I would later find out that they were for my benefit. I felt like it was unreasonable for my leader to tell me to read at least three books a month, but it was for my benefit. He was protecting me from ignorance and slothfulness. He desired to fill my unproductive time with something that was useful and beneficial. Submission can be difficult mainly because you don't understand it, but it is important that you remain submitted anyway.

There have been instances where my wife and I did not agree on the direction of some things. We are both very strong people. When we have a way we desire to go, there isn't anyone or anything that can detour us. We've had to learn the art of submitting ourselves to one way instead of trying to go different ways. I don't subscribe to the idea that the husband is always right. It sounds great, but it isn't realistic. Wives are not property, and they should not be treated as inanimate objects without the capability of being wise and productive. Therefore, I am quick to seek confirmation when choosing a direction from my wife, as she is my helpmeet. I must remember that God gave me a helpmeet to help me. That would make the most sense. The problem arises when it is time for one of us to bow the knee.

I am thankful for a wife who respects me enough to submit to my way, but I do not make it a practice of assuming my way is always right. Instead, I weigh the evidence she brings to me before making a decision. Ultimately, I believe God blesses the decision because we willingly submit to it and because we believe it is the way He desires for us to go. We remain protected that way.

At the beginning of our marriage, my wife wanted to start an organization, but I was not in agreement with it. I felt like it was a great idea, but it was too soon. Neither of us was at a place we needed to be, and I communicated it to her. She became frustrated with me because she felt like I was trying to contain the vision God gave her. That wasn't it at all. I wanted to protect her from shame and embarrassment. While the vision was great, it was not ready to be built. I could not sit back as a husband and watch my wife build something that I knew she could not finish.

After a very heated argument about her vision, my wife made it seem like she was going to do it anyway. I became very upset and said to her, "Well, you do it then! I won't cover it! You'll be by yourself!" I stormed out the bedroom to the living room to sit down while she remained in the bedroom. About two hours later she came into the living room and sat next to me. "Babe, I'm not going to do it. I couldn't imagine stepping outside your protection because of rebellion." I was overjoyed and thankful for a wife who understood this benefit of submission. She started the organization a year later, and today, it serves thousands of women all over the world.

It can seem hard to serve under a pastor who tries to contain your gifts and abilities. It's tough because you assume he actually has that authority to do so. Let me set you free from something. Your pastor does not have that much power. No person in authority can stop God's plans for your life. The judge cannot overturn God's will for you. The lawyer cannot bring any evidence against God's will for you. Your boss cannot fire you from it. What God has predestined for you is for you. You must trust Him.

Instead of looking at your pastor as someone trying to stifle or contain your gifts, ask yourself what is God trying to teach you during this time. What is the lesson you need to learn? I advised a young man against a couple of things He wanted to begin. He was unsure as to the timing of his projects, and he sat down with me for wisdom. Although he is gifted greatly, his character could not sustain even the smallest amount of success. I encouraged him to focus on his character instead of trying to build a ministry that would embarrass him later on. He became very upset with me, and he started the ministry anyways. I sought to protect him from what I could foresee. Unfortunately, he did not heed my advice.

What's always puzzling is having these young men sit down with me searching for wisdom and watching them go the opposite direction. They are quick to believe they are submitted until I tell them "No!" That one answer is enough to expose the heart of men and women. I am loved and cherished when I tell people "Yes," but I am usually hated and abandoned the moment I say "No!"

The young man started the ministry, and he saw a little success from it. Some people started giving towards it. Unfortunately, he took all of the money and wasted it in sinful living. He was ultimately embarrassed by it and has yet to recover from the shame. He felt like I was trying to hold him back from it instead of seeing that I had his best interest at heart. I desired, and still desire, for him to succeed. Therefore, I told him the truth to save him from shame. He rebelled against it, but he learned a valuable lesson because of it.

You must understand there is a great benefit in submitting to your spiritual leaders. I don't take a "no" as a bad thing anymore. In fact, I have gotten to a point in my life and ministry that I enjoy the "no." I enjoy it because I know God is protecting me from something that I don't know about. And I am not quick to get something that could destroy me. I'd rather wait and get it in its appropriate time. If you have bitterness in your heart against your pastor, get rid of it immediately! That's the enemy trying to get you unprotected. The same goes for your marriage or on your job. Get back in line under the protection God has ordained for you.

If you do not have a pastor or covering, I would highly recommend you find one. Many people shy away from it because they want to do what they want to do. They cannot take criticism, so they become islands unto themselves. You cannot afford it. I have what I like to call a pocket of accountability. It is made up of pastors who are much older and wiser than I am. They are responsible for guiding and rebuking me. I have determined in my heart that I will submit to these men even if I don't feel as if their words are the best for me. I submit because I must and choose to. It is for my protection.

Submission is also an act of great strength. Any fool can rebel. It takes strength to submit. When you hear the word 'submit' what do you typically think? Weakness? Passivity? Slavery? Our society pushes a doctrine of rebellion. We do not like to submit to anyone or anything. Many work hard to be their "own person" and make their "own way." Many rebel against their boss, their spouse, their pastor, their parents, and their Lord. We live in a culture of entitlement that is all about having the right to do whatever you want to do. It's hedonism at its finest. Many want to eat it, drink it, smoke it, romance it, snort it, say it, resent it, and love it without being told what is right or wrong.

This idea becomes tougher for women, who are confronted with messages of worldly feminism. It's the idea that women do not need men for anything. That they run the world and all that is in it. While some preach a message of equality, they negate any kind of order in the workplace, home, or the church. Since many do not understand the true definition of submission, they assume that it's about being passive and weak. That is simply not true. According to the biblical definition, which is to yield or surrender oneself to the will or authority of another, he or she who surrenders has control. In fact, he or she has great power. This individual is independent in their power, which means they have full authority in how they will lend this authority to someone else. If he chooses to submit, then it means he surrenders under his own free will to the will of another authority.

When the scripture says for wives to submit to their husbands, it implies that the wife has an independent authority and strength. She must make a positive decision to lend her authority to her husband for order and peace in the home. Luckily, wives and husbands have an opportunity to submit to one another out of reverence for Christ, which is Ephesians 5:21. I mentioned how my wife and I do this in an earlier paragraph. There must be times when one chooses to bow the knee or release his or her authority for peace and order. There cannot be two paths. One must submit to the other. Ultimately, submission is an act of strength. When my wife got a revelation of this, she realized just how strong she was.

Do not be fooled into thinking that you are weak because you choose to submit to your pastor. Only the foolish and rebellious will chastise you because of your willingness to do it. Remain strong, and continue to submit. And remember that submission is your willingness to surrender; slavery is being beaten into surrender.

Submission is also for your training. I wish I understood this pillar of submission years ago. We've established that you must get under the mission of another. Submission to your pastor or spiritual authority is critical. Allowing for him to help lead and guide you in truth is paramount to your development. First Timothy 3:2-4 reminds us that an overseer must be a man whose life is above reproach. He must be faithful to his wife, exercise self-control, live wisely, and have a good reputation. He enjoys guests in his home and must be able to teach. He should not be a heavy drinker or violent. He is gentle, not quarrelsome, and not a lover of money. He manages his family well, with children who respect and obey him. These are the standards you look for in a covering. If your covering, or pastor, does not exemplify those qualities, then it is safe to say that you should look elsewhere.

God gives us spiritual leaders for the purpose of edification. It is their job to edify or build us up, so we can do the work of the ministry. If you are already a spiritual leader, you understand the weight that you carry. We are responsible for training those individuals God places in our care. Hebrews 13:17 reads, "Obey your spiritual leaders, and do what they say. Their work is to watch over your souls, and they are accountable to God. Give them reason to do this with joy and not with sorrow. That would certainly not be for your benefit." You don't want your pastor to see you as a burden. You do not want to be that difficult student the teacher dreads being around.

I love everyone God has placed under my leadership, but there are some that I do not always look forward to seeing. I ask God to work on my heart concerning it. As the verse states, I watch over them with sorrow, not joy, and it is not to their benefit. I see so much potential in them, but they are hard-headed. They desire my "yes" and despise my "no." They hear what I say, but they refuse to listen to the point of obedience. They act out of emotion and do not consider their actions. I can talk to them until I am blue in the face, but nothing really changes. It is as if they have set their heart to rebel. It's sad to watch someone walk down that road especially those with children and a spouse. I can understand taking yourself down a rebellious path, but why would you want to subject your spouse and children to it? It's unfortunate.

As a pastor, I desire to pour into and train those under my leadership. I want them to be better than me. I love to see them excel for the cause of Christ. I am not afraid to challenge them or rebuke them whenever necessary. It is for their growth and maturity. I will give every resource I have to assist them. That is the heart of a pastor to those under his care. I implore you to submit to your spiritual leader and receive the training that is presented to you. And do not think that your most valuable training will be in a classroom.

I learned the most in earlier ministry assignments while I was moving chairs, walking door-to-door with the evangelism team, helping to sweep the bathroom because the pastor couldn't afford a professional company to clean, and so much more. It was on-the-job training for me, and it was needed. You need it as well. You could be assigned to work out in the parking lot. If that's the need of the local body that's where you should be. My advice is to be the best parking lot assistant you can be. Look for ways to do it better, and have it in your mind that you desire to ease the burden for your pastor.

We moved our church three times in one year. It was stressful. We finally found a new temporary space that was perfect for us. We have a great need for parking lot attendants to assist the people parking their cars and finding the sanctuary. So, you can see why this example is on my mind!

After several weeks announcing it, we had our first service. I asked my executive pastor how many men signed up to assist, and he told me no one did. Instead of being upset, I did what any leader would do in that situation—stepped up to the plate myself and got out in the parking lot. I showed up to the church a couple of hours early to make sure everything was setup properly. I grabbed our signs and went to the entrance of the parking lot. As cars drove in, they looked shocked. Some stopped, rolled their windows down, and took a picture. They couldn't believe their pastor was standing out in the parking lot making sure they parked properly. My goal was to show the men what they could and should have stepped up to the plate to do. Many men got out of the car, walked their spouse and children into church, and came out to help. I gave them a vest and instructed them on what they should do. After a couple of weeks of leading them in the parking lot, the men had it. They were arriving early to serve. One of the men said to me, "I felt horrible knowing that my pastor was in the parking lot. I knew there were so many other things you could have been doing." He was right, but my most important job at that time was showing the people that I could serve them in the parking lot, as well as, the sanctuary. I was training them on the fly.

The lesson in servanthood they learned out in the parking lot was greater than what they could have been taught in the sanctuary. In fact, those men have heard me preach about servanthood before. They needed to see and experience it for themselves. You will remain in this position for your entire journey. If you ever get to a point where you think you know more than your leader and it causes you to be disrespectful, either fix your heart or leave. The enemy will use you to poison the organization. If you cannot serve with cheerfulness where you are and develop beyond your emotions, then it is better for you to leave.

You will also have to watch out for becoming too familiar. Don't allow for your closeness or connection to your spiritual leader to cause you to disrespect him. When your spiritual leader ceases from being pastor to just some man who preaches on the weekend, then you have lost respect. Being too familiar will cause you to rebel. This is because you can't be familiar and submissive. You must keep it in your mind that your spiritual leader deserves your respect. God placed you under his care for a reason.

I know how this happens and how it destroys because I became a victim of it. I've been on both sides. There was a time that I became so familiar with my spiritual leaders that I did not respect their office or wisdom. I referred to one of my pastors as John. He was just John. He wanted us to call him John, but I did not really understand submission and authority at that time. After calling him John over and over again, I slowly saw him as just another sheep in the pasture. I failed to see him as the undershepherd he was. He was the pastor of the church; therefore, he was given charge to watch over my soul. I did not give him that respect.

When my perspective of the pastor changed, my respect for him dwindled. That created a toxic environment. The more familiar I became, the less honor and respect I had for him. One of the worst things that could have happened was when I saw my pastor at his most vulnerable moments. I was too immature to know how to respond to him. I also saw him in his most intense moments.

Ham, one of Noah's sons, saw him naked and passed out in his drunkenness. After seeing him, he told his other two brothers, Shem and Japheth. They covered their father with a cloth to uphold his integrity in his moment of weakness. They refused to look at him in his humiliation. Sadly, it was a member of Noah's family who ran to tell others of his indiscretions instead of covering him from his shame and weakness. Many take this story and pervert it. I've heard other pastors tell those who serve them that they should look, but not respond. They seek to cover the nakedness of their pastor without praying or responding in some way to bring restoration. I do not believe in watching someone continue in sin without repentance. I do not care what title he has. That should never be tolerated. However, we must never be like Ham and run to tell others about our spiritual leader's weaknesses and vulnerabilities. That is wrong and dishonorable.

No matter how angry you become, you must never strike the one God has placed over you. David shows us this in 1 Samuel 26:9-11. He was anointed to be the future king, but the current king, Saul, desired to kill him. He threw a spear at David, ordered soldiers to take him, and chased him into a mountainous cave. Even through all of that, David responds by saying, "I will not touch God's anointed. Who can touch God's anointed and be guiltless? Verses 9-11 reads

> 'No!' David said. 'Don't kill him. For who can remain innocent after attacking the LORD's anointed one? Surely the LORD will strike Saul down someday, or he will die of old age or in battle. The LORD forbid that I should kill the one he has anointed! But take his spear and that jug of water beside his head, and then let's get out of here!'

David realized that he would be guilty before God if he touched God's anointed. David realized something that's important for you to realize—God placed your spiritual leaders in their position whether you like what they do or not. They are God's anointed, and you should revere and respect them. They are assigned to train you, and you must realize that the training will be different from what you assume it should be. Either way, submit to it.

God desires for you to submit to be trained, to be humbled, to be protected, and to showcase your strength. Don't rebel against the process. You will be tempted to do so. Don't take the bait.

THEY CANNOT GO ANY FURTHER

It is honorable to desire that others go where you are going. Unfortunately, that is not always possible. Leadership demands an adequate and responsible amount of separation. At times, this separation is brought on by thought-out decisions. Other times, it happens due to certain situations and unfortunate circumstances. Nevertheless, it is vital for the health of the organization and the sustainability of the leader. It must be understood that some people within your organization cannot go any further. Where you are right now is where the line must be drawn. If they go any further within your organization, it could stunt its growth and overall productivity.

In Genesis 12, God called Abram to leave the ruling order he was under, his relatives, and his native country to journey to a land God was going to show him. God spoke clearly to Abram, and He gave him a vision. I believe this happened with you as well. God spoke to you and gave you a vision. It was that initial vision that started your journey to building your organization. This part of the journey is very important. The people will perish without a proper, workable vision. They must know that you have heard from God. They need to know you had your burning bush experience where God encountered you, spoke to you, and gave you instructions. This is important, and it cannot be overlooked!

Abram had the vision. God said to him in Genesis 12:2-3 (NLT), "I will make you into a great nation. I will bless you and make you famous, and you will be a blessing to others. I will bless those who bless you and curse those who treat you with contempt. All the families on earth will be blessed through you." This vision is not only a central theme of what Abram was called to do, but it speaks to his overall existence. It also shows that the vision of what he was to become was larger than what he could see. Simply put, Abram was the vessel that would ultimately benefit others. I pray that you see your organization the same way. It is the vessel God will use to bring deliverance, peace, and prosperity to others.

As I believe you have done, Abram left as the Lord instructed him, but his nephew, Lot, went with him. Someone traveling with you is a two-fold complexity. Initially, you must allow the other person to go with you. Secondly, the other person must be willing to go with you. These are important aspects of leadership. Those who serve alongside you must be carefully selected and must have a willingness to go with you. They need to see and understand the vision. They don't have to know all the details, but they need to know enough of it so they can perform their responsibilities, which ultimately helps the overall progression of the organization. Having competent, able people to assist you in accomplishing the vision is important. However, never get so entangled in the lives of those who serve alongside you that you believe their entire life is purposed to just serve with you. Many great leaders have left great organizations. Their leaving does not discredit the organization. Neither does it devalue them. Sometimes, people have to leave to fulfill the will God has for them.

Everything has an expiration date, and change can be good. Understanding these universal principles is paramount to seeing sustainable growth. We know from Genesis 13:5 that Lot became very wealthy because of his association with Abram. He had flocks of sheep and goats, herds of cattle, and many tents. He was so wealthy in possessions that the land he was on with his uncle, Abram, was not large enough to support them both. Due to the tightness of space, arguments started breaking out between the servants in the two camps.

Abram stood and responded to the disputes with wisdom. He said to his nephew in Genesis 13:8, 9,

> Let's not allow this conflict to come between us or our herdsmen. After all, we are close relatives! The whole countryside is open to you. Take your choice of any section of the land you want, and we will separate. If you want the land to the left, then I'll take the land on the right. If you prefer the land on the right, then I'll go to the left.

Abram did something very few leaders do—he diffused the situation by being open-minded and generous. Any strong leader should desire for his employees and servant-leaders to flourish. I know I do. I want to help them thrive. I feel as though God sends people to my organization and leadership to assist them in their development. I want to see them excel, not decline.

Like Abram did with Lot, I notice the personal aspect of leadership. Abram understood that the problem was much larger than just a few herdsmen arguing over land. Therefore, he said, "...we are close relatives!" They were relatives, and I do understand that you are not related to many of the servant-leaders and employees in your organization. However, you must realize that leadership is personal. It could be that your secretary is not well-equipped to do the job. She cannot focus on her responsibilities because she is having problems at home. No, you probably cannot fix them, but simply showing you care would be more than enough to encourage her to put appropriate effort into her work.

Leaders must understand the relationship between personal connection and productivity. I always remind my servant-leaders that their decisions will influence others. I want them to see the crying faces and happy smiles from our parishioners. That is important to me because I want them to realize that their service is not unto me. I am the leader, but they are serving the people directly. I want them personally connected to their work. I want them to have a sense of pride for their outcomes so they can focus on their output.

Making work personal will always increase productivity. When there is no connection, productivity decreases. I remind people that the church I pastor is our church, not my church. After they understand that principle, I remind them that our church is also their church. They take ownership, which ultimately increases attendance and productivity. When you have an investment in something, you usually treat it a little better.

It was on that plot of land that Abram realized he and his nephew could not go any further. I am sure there are some people in your organization that cannot go any further. They excelled and progressed with you, but this is the end of the road. For some of the people, it is a relief to know that they are leaving. This is because they are the trouble-makers. They complain, murmur, gossip, and are never satisfied with anything. Peace will arise the moment they depart. For others, it is not that easy.

I have had many people walk into my life only to have to release them to go somewhere else. That part is hard. You do not want to let them go, but it is needed and profitable for the entire organization. If you do not let them go there will be contention, and some will spread the venom to others. The infected must be removed before they infect others.

Please do not take this lightly! They are very contagious. Let them go before they ruin what you have worked hard to build. The longer they stay, the more mischief they will spread. I know that because I made this mistake too many times. I felt like I could change some of them, but I found out the hard way that their hardened heart was not mendable. I felt sorry for some of them because I knew letting them go would mean they would not have anything. I had to learn that I was not their god. They could not trust in me. Finally, I tried to convince the rabble rousers to settle down and connect with their work. However, I had to learn that I could not persuade them to connect to their work. They have to do that themselves.

Allowing people the opportunity to leave is important. It is important for them and for the organization. If you have a group of complainers and agitators, it is important to let them go. Make it clear that this is the furthest they can go.

And unfortunately, this the furthest I'm going with you right now. I pray you have been edified and encouraged to continue on in faith. Please remember that God's hand is on you, separation is inevitable, tests will come, trials must be endured, and God's will must be done.

Remain encouraged and eternity focused. This life is bigger than you. You are His vessel, set aside for His purpose and tasked with bringing Him glory. Welcome to the fold—a natural group of men and women tasked with an extraordinary assignment and equipped with supernatural wisdom and authority. Welcome.

ABOUT THE AUTHOR

Cornelius Lindsey (born August 16, 1986) is an American trailblazer, husband, father, pastor, author, and entrepreneur. He is the Founder and Senior Pastor of The Gathering Oasis Church, a non-denominational church located in the Greater Atlanta area. He is the author of ten books, most notably *When God's Hand is on You*, *So You Want to Be a Man?*, *I'm Married. Now, What?*, and *The Imperfect Family Man*. Other aspects of Lindsey's ministry include his annual men's conference; the non-profit organization, "The Man Cave Society;" and his podcast, "Real Life with Cornelius Lindsey" which airs weekly talks on Christian manhood, fatherhood, and leadership. His social media has drawn nearly 500,000 followers, and his conferences bring together men and women from countries around the world.

In October 2009, after a stint in politics, Lindsey accepted his God-given call to pastor. After three years of diligent prayer, Lindsey and his wife Heather founded The Gathering Oasis Church. The church's first service was held on January 28, 2013. In addition to his local ministry, Cornelius Lindsey has become a prominent guest speaker in the United States and internationally. His speaking engagements have spanned across the globe to Jamaica, the Bahamas, London, Asia, and Africa.

As a preacher, Cornelius' passionate, high-impact, and straightforward approach is exactly what is needed to propel men and women to advance the Gospel.

Cornelius and Heather are the proud parents of two children, Logan and Taylor. They currently reside in the quiet suburbs of Atlanta, GA. In his spare time, Cornelius enjoys keeping tabs on politics and sweating in the gym.

––––––––––––––––––––––––––––––––––

The two greatest moments of your life are the day you are born again and the day you realize you are living in a graveyard of potential. You have been chosen and called by God for a reason. You were created with purpose on purpose for a purpose. He has placed His hand on you for His will. This book helps you to understand what it means to have God's hand on you. Cornelius answers these important questions:

What does it mean to be called into ministry?
How do you begin in ministry?
Does God call us to prepare and train?
Should we be submitted to authority before starting in ministry?
Will I need to overcome my insecurities before continuing in ministry?

It is time for you to walk in your calling. You have been touched by God to serve His people, and someone is waiting for you to walk in your purpose. There are people on the other side of your obedience. Don't keep them waiting! God's hand is on you.

Made in the USA
San Bernardino, CA
22 August 2017